In What
Light There Is

Linda Flashinski

For Sue — My Forever Friend — Linda

ISBN: 1505282373
ISBN 13: 9781505282375
Library of Congress Control Number: 2014921465
CreateSpace Independent Publishing Platform
North Charleston, South Carolina

"And still, I look at this world
As worlds will be seen -
In what light there is..."

John Ciardi

About the Author

Linda Flashinski has worked as an educator, social service agency associate director, school district administrator, radio host, columnist, presenter, community volunteer, and writer. She is a mother and grandmother and resides in Caledonia, Wisconsin with her husband. She has a degree from UW-Madison and her work has appeared in the Journal Times, the Milwaukee Journal Sentinel, Copycat Magazine, Pockets, and other publications. She can be reached at lindaflashinski@hotmail.com.

Dedicated to our dear children,
Rachel, Todd, Jocelyn, and Jeff,
And to our precious grandchildren.

Note to Readers.....

In What Light There Is represents a collection of some of the essays and columns I have written over the years. These reflections explore the issues affecting our times and our lives with subjects such as hope, justice, human rights, growing older, Alzheimer's, courage, and even the deep tragedy of losing a child. I send these words out, hoping that they speak to the bittersweet nature of the journey we travel with its great joys and its great sorrows.

There are two recurring themes in the history of Literature that are compelling to me. One is the interconnectedness of all beings, and the mystery of that inexplicable bond. There is a profound quote about that connection by Francis Thompson (1859-1907). *"All things....to each other so linked are/that thou canst not stir a flower/without troubling a star."*

Another compelling theme is the interplay of light and darkness, ultimately suggesting that it is somewhere between darkness and light that we view the world. Thus, this volume is akin to a series of snapshots which we see, as John Ciardi wrote, *"as worlds will be seen....in what light there is."*

Table of Contents

Tributes, And Beyond

Author's Parents, circa 1941

"At times our own light goes out and is rekindled by a spark from another person. Each of us has cause to think with deep gratitude of those who have lighted the flame within us."
— Albert Schweitzer

A Father's Gift

The day before my father died of a painful cancer, the nurses had to move him from a bed to a gurney. In doing so, they lost their grip of him and dropped him onto the hard gurney. In pain, he let out a strangled groan. But that's not what those of us who loved him remember most about the incident. What we remember most is that, within moments of being dropped, my father, kind and gentle to the end, turned to the nurses and said, "Oh, dearies, you do such a good job. Thank you for being here to help me." In his agony, he was worried about what distress his mournful groan may have caused others.

That was my father. During the difficult days of growing up in a world where we fail so often, he was just the antidote to self-deprecation and self-despair that we needed. When we did poorly on a test, when we lost a game, when we stumbled in some more painful, personal area of our lives, he would just smile his smile and assure us that we were really special, that things would be all right, that this, too, would pass. And it always did, in time. What never did pass was the sense we got from him and from my mother that the ground we walked on was safe and sure, that we could believe in ourselves, and that we could help others in this complicated journey because we had been so helped in our growing up years.

I was reminded of the hospital incident last year over the holidays when I was at the post office, waiting in line. The line was long and, even though the three postal workers were diligently attending to their work, the cordon of people had backed up. People shuffled and finally a man behind me said, loudly enough for everyone to hear, including the postal workers, "Well, isn't this the U.S. government at work? Just more incompetence for our tax dollars." Several people mumbled agreement.

I looked at the postal workers who continued stamping and sorting and giving change and smiling and saying "thank you," and they didn't flinch. Still, it must have hurt. My mind flashed back to my father who, being dropped onto a gurney, was able, even in pain, to turn to others who had failed and to tell them that he knew that they were doing the best they could in a trying situation. I thought of his ability to see that most of us are just out here, struggling for the light that is often elusive, succeeding sometimes and failing other times, and being what we are – human and imperfect and growing with each mistake and each success.

We live in an age besieged with critics and complainers, with those who tell us what is wrong with everything – what is wrong with the younger generation, what is wrong with the older generation, what is wrong with liberals, what is wrong with conservatives, what is wrong with women, what is wrong with men, and, always, what is wrong with the government.

In this backdrop, it is intriguing to consider what the world would be like if more people looked to see what is good and strong and right around us. For surely, we see it every day. A government providing roads and trash pickup and immunizations and free public education. Young people working in school, striving toward productive and caring futures. Senior citizens serving as mentors and tutors to the young. Volunteers in virtually every organization asking how they can help. And children whose eyes, despite the problems of our times, still reflect light and love and hope and tomorrow.

It is not easy to be human. Sometimes we speak too harshly to our children or to our parents or to our spouse. Sometimes we fail at our job. Sometimes we don't add up the accounts accurately. Sometimes we give a test that is too difficult. Sometimes we don't study enough. Sometimes we prescribe a medication that doesn't work. Sometimes we take the order down incorrectly. And sometimes we drop an ill, elderly patient onto a gurney. Sometimes, despite our best intentions, we just plain do it wrong.

But imagine what a world it would be if, in the face of someone else's mistake, we remembered our own shortcomings and considered what it is to be human.

Imagine what a world it would be if we told others with our actions, our words, our eyes, that we know that they are who we are – all too human and trying, just the same, to do what we can in "what light there is."

All That I Am

"All that I am, or ever hope to be, I owe to my angel mother," wrote Abraham Lincoln. I think of his words and that quote each May as we celebrate our own mothers.

My mother is gone almost a decade now. She was a bright and strong woman at a time when brightness and strength were not necessarily the most desired traits in women. But strong she was, and passionate about the issues in our country and in our world. After she passed away, we found among her things copies of the numerous letters she had written over the years to various legislators and leaders and US Presidents. She made sure her voice was heard. To her, it was what you do in a democracy.

My mother was the first activist I ever encountered. She was also the first person I knew who opposed the Vietnam War, even before students or politicians or other activists were speaking out. I remember her saying that the United States would pay a terrible price for years to come for our involvement in that war. I was in high school at the time and there hadn't been much talk yet in the general public about the war, so she was prophetic in her words. Historians note that Vietnam was the beginning of our loss of faith in institutions and the beginning of a loss of innocence in our country.

In the years after my mom's first prophetic words, the problems of Vietnam became more apparent and much debated. I was a student at UW-Madison by then, and was among the many who protested the war, who marched, and who worked for Eugene McCarthy and his anti-war platform. I will never forget the passion of so many of us against that war, against napalming, against what we considered to be an illegal and immoral intrusion. And, like my mother and the other idealists back then, I hoped and dreamed that our nation would take a more humane stance in our actions around the globe, and that we would live by our finest principles. We not only wanted peace, but we wanted justice for minorities, equality for women, and civil rights for all. Much negative is written of the youth culture of the time, but what I remember always about that time is the pure idealism. We believed that our nation could live by higher standards.

That's a long way of saying that my mother and others knew about the energy it takes to fight for what is right, to speak out against wrongdoing, and to never sit by passively without letting your voice be heard. Speak truth to power, my mom always believed. I am proud for any part of that which remains alive inside of me.

For all of her activism, my mother was a person at peace. She and my dad lived in a middle class neighborhood in a big white house with pear trees and apple trees and even, for a while, grape vines. I'll never forget the warm apple pies of fall or the sweet pear and grape jams of summer that my mother made with the fruits of the earth. My mom and dad were happy people who appreciated their home, adored their children, and laughed a great deal. They lived life easy and they were gentle parents. They seemed to feel as Lincoln did when he said, "I have always found that mercy bears richer fruits than strict justice." Gentleness and humor resonated within the walls of their home.

Years later, after the deaths of my parents, we sold their big white house to a young couple who fell in love with it. The passion of that couple made us feel as if the sale was meant to be. That feeling was re-enforced in the months afterwards when we happened past the house and saw an anti-Iraq war sign in the front yard. We decided that our mother would have been smiling.

Strength was not the only gift my mother had. She was compassionate, and perhaps that was one of the reasons why needless wars bothered her so much. She was also very grateful for the fullness of her life. When I was a young mother she said, "Enjoy these days. They go by so quickly." I think those words are the reason I write so often of the poignant beauty and brief-ness of this journey. It is such a gift.

One of the best legacies my mother left me was her gift of words. She kept loose leaf notebooks of writings and quotes she liked, and she would often share articles or books with me. I know that my mother's early encouragement of reading played an enormous part in all of the words that rattle around in my gray matter.

No one is and no one has the perfect, idealized mother of story and song. But maybe on Mother's Day and throughout the year we can, like Lincoln, reflect on the good things in our mothers who did the best they could within the circumstances of their lives. To them, we owe much of "what we are or ever hope to be."

So, if your mother is still with you, now is a good time to give her a word of thanks for whatever strengths she possesses that live inside of you.

And if your mother is here only in spirit, send her a little word nonetheless.

For she lives on in pear jams or in warm apple pies or in stirring words or in passionate spirits. Or in whatever her gift to you was, large or small.

And so every May, I send a little word myself.

Happy Mothers Day, Mom.

I miss you.

The Foolish Ones

Steven Jobs passed away on October 5, 2011. He was only 56 years of age. The world was stunned by the news, even though we had known of his cancer diagnosis, his weight loss, and his recent resignation from Apple. Still, it was a shock. Steve Jobs was a hero and a visionary, one who imagined a future and then created it. And he began in a simple way, working out of his garage with his friend Steve Wozniak. He did it by making calls from his bedroom phone to sell the computers they created. And he did it years ago at a time when many still wondered what anyone would even do with computers in their homes. "How would we use them?," they asked themselves back in those more innocent days. Still, Jobs saw the possibilities and, young and foolish, he took a chance with his gift of imagination and it changed the world.

In 2005, Steven Jobs spoke to the graduating class at Stanford University and reflected on his life experiences and their meaning. And he had three profound messages for those graduates and for us.

His first message was a reminder in life to "connect the dots." He spoke of his dropping out of college and of stumbling into so many opportunities that would form his future, such as taking a calligraphy class that would later impact on the typography of computer design. "Much of what I stumbled into by following my curiosity and intuition turned out to be priceless later on," he told the graduates. He told them that their dots of action would connect in the future if they followed their hearts even when their journey was "off the well-worn path."

His second message stemmed from his experience of being fired from Apple when he was 30 years old, fired from the very company he began. As painful as that was, over time he came to the slow realization that, for all that had happened to him, he was still in love with his work. That realization led him to the world of animation and the founding of Pixar, one of the most successful animation companies in the world. And so his second message was hard-won and deep. "The only way to do great work," he said, "is to love what you do."

And his third message was about death and was strangely prophetic. "Death is the destination we all share," he reminded his young audience. And it is, he went on to say, "the best invention of life" since it reminds us that our time here is limited, and that we need to follow our hearts. He spoke of a quote he loved from the Whole Earth Catalog. "Stay hungry. Stay foolish." He said he never forgot those words.

It makes us wonder if those who change the world share this sense of using their gifts, this sense of staying foolish, and this sense of understanding the briefness of our journey here.

For there have been foolish ones throughout time.

There was Amelia Earhart who, after working as a nurse on an airfield decided that "I knew I had to fly." By doing what many viewed as foolish at the time, she became a role model for the thousands of women who would later become aviators, some serving as transport pilots in WWII. "When a great adventure is offered," Amelia later said, "one dare not refuse it."

There was Luciano Pavarotti who was working as an insurance salesman when he, some at the time said, foolishly decided to leave his job to take voice lessons to see what he could do with his talent. And so we got to hear that incredible, resonating tenor and the unbelievable gift that his voice gave to the world.

There was Jim Henson, the wonder-filled, creative artist who decided to embrace his foolishness and focus his life's work on puppets, thus creating words, songs, movies, and philosophy that would resonate through time. As Kermit could be saying of Henson, "We've done just what we set out to do, thanks to the lovers, the dreamers, and you."

There was Mother Teresa, that giving, loving spirit who made the decision to devote her life to work among the poorest of the world and so became a role model of how much good can be done in this life by one person. "In life," she said, "we can do no great things. We can only do small things with great love."

Steven Jobs, Luciano Pavarotti, Amelia Earhart, Jim Henson, Mother Teresa, Leonardo Da Vinci, Mark Twain, Jane Addams, Thomas Edison, and all of those who challenge themselves remind us of a truth often pushed aside in the routine of our days. The world is forever transformed when talents become unleashed, when we embrace our own foolishness, when we use our gifts.

And what does the world gain by it?

The world gains Steven Jobs' imagination and, with it, computers and I-Pods and animation and connectedness, and the fullness of possibilities for the future. The world gains Amelia Earhart's adventurousness and, with it, women who understand their own possibilities. The world gains Pavarotti's voice and, with it, a deeper understanding of opera, of music, of passion, and of life. The world gains Jim Henson's creativity and, with it, Muppets, humor, song, movies, and a sense of life's joy and beauty. The world gains Mother Teresa's compassion and, with it, an understanding of how much we can help those in need through our own simple actions.

Yes, what happens when we use that which we are given is a wondrous thing. It may be a grand imagination, a moving voice, words on paper, paint on canvas, a generosity of spirit, or any of the diverse gifts that exist in this complex journey.

Perhaps the life of Steven Jobs will help us toward some introspection, some sense that the time is now for each of us to unwrap the gifts that we have to give. As Jobs himself reminded us, this sweet journey we are on is an exquisitely beautiful and a terribly brief one. Maybe it is time for all of our voices to be heard.

There were multiple flowers and notes left at Apple stores across the country as memorial tributes when Steven Jobs passed away. One of those notes read, "This is for the foolish ones, the ones who change the world."

Indeed.

Bending the Tree

Dear Educators,
The bell rings.
The classroom door opens.
It is the first day of the school year and in they come, our children.

 * He sits in the front row of your third grade class, and he smiles shyly at you, an eager-to-be-here look on his face, holding his feet out stiffly in his brand new white Nike shoes. His mom is president of the PTA at your school. And he is our child.

 * She sits in her stained shirt with the rip at the shoulder, and you wonder at her bruises, and her haunted eyes, and her unspoken sadness. And she is our child.

 * He is in your biology class, and he is bright and creative, and not achieving to his potential, and he doodles when he should be doing his labs. And he is our child.

 * She can barely stay awake in your parenting class. She works too late at night at a part-time job, and lately her figure bulges at her waist. You think you know why. She is just 15 years old. And she is our child.

 * He raises his hand for Student Council, and for carrying the flag, and for being in the school play, and for singing in the choir, and for entering the math contest. He will always be there, right up in front of his class. And he is our child.

* He pokes the girl in front of him, and causes fights on the playground and drops books when you are trying to teach. Last week he was in detention. His phone is unlisted, and no one answers your notes. And he is our child.

* She goes home to a house in the suburbs where the table is already set for supper. Her bedroom has a four-poster bed with a Little Mermaid bedspread. And she is our child.

* She goes home to a house with broken windows and a smell of urine and a wealth of mice. The mattress she sleeps on leans against a wall and when she sleeps, she falls asleep to the sound of gunshots from a nearby playground. And she is our child.

* She is class secretary and valedictorian and a Big Sister and she gets three scholarships to go to college. And she is our child.

* He has a knife in his pocket today, and he gets suspended. He will now be transferred to his third high school in a year and a half. And he is our child.

And we send them all to you. The lucky ones, museumed and lessoned and nurtured. And the unlucky ones, neglected and alienated and abused.

We send them all to you, 25% in poverty, 6.5 million requiring special education services out of a national school population of 58 million.

We send them all to you.

And we don't ask much of you. Just to help them read. And work with figures. And spell their words.

No, we don't ask much of you. Just to teach them history. And a little algebra. And to be strong enough to stay away from gangs.

No, we don't ask much of you. Just to hold them when they cry. And pull their loose teeth to send home for the tooth fairy, and to be their mentors.

No, we don't ask much of you. Just to counsel them as teenagers about drinking, and abuse, and pregnancy and AIDS.

No, we don't ask much of you. Just to teach them to drive a car and use computers and get along with others of all cultures.

No, we don't ask much of you. Just to get them ready for college, or get them ready for a trade. Just to teach them not to give in to hopelessness.

No, we don't ask much of you. Just to watch over 30 elementary school children for seven hours a day, or to try to know 150 high school students well enough to help them. Just to be slow to anger and quick to understanding even when your feet are tired.

No, we don't ask much of you. Just to touch a life. Just to make a difference. Just to bend the tree of the future a little more toward sunlight.

And to know how much we thank you for all we ask of you.

Thanks for Giving

On a recent morning in this season of Thanksgiving, I was reflecting on the things I am grateful for when I noticed our dog Toby moving cautiously down the stairs. I realized again how old he has gotten, nearly ninety years of age in human time. These days, he sleeps more, walks more slowly, and doesn't see so well. I think how much we will miss him when he leaves us. He is a gentle dog who keeps us company in a house that is often quiet now that our four children are grown. I am grateful for him, this pal of our own aging years.

I think back to the first dog we had in the busy days of our young growing family, and I remember how much joy he brought to us, too. I remember also his aging years, and the day that he died. In the weeks before his death, he had turned into a bony skeleton of himself. His last attempt to eat, one week prior, was followed by a terrible bout of nausea. He had almost quit drinking, too, and would only lap a little water when I carried the bowl to him. The morning of his death, he was not even able to push himself up on his skinny legs. I called the vet who said that giving him a shot was the only merciful choice we had. And so I wrapped his tiny frame into a blanket, said a gentle goodbye to him, and traveled with him to the veterinary clinic. It was time, and I knew it. So did he, I think. He was given a shot, and he went to sleep in my arms, not a whimper out of him.

I, who had always been opposed to this kind of euthanasia, who had thought that all beings should die naturally, was changed by experience. My little friend was suffering, with a suffering he would never escape from. I was able to mercifully deliver him, and I did. He is buried in the woods behind our home under a rock that reads, "To our beloved friend, Rags. We will always miss you."

It is true that a part of me still misses Rags. He was his own person, a dog who came to us at three years of age, damaged by early abuse, but willing to learn to trust again in exchange for basic fairness. We took the deal, surrounded him with affection, and he paid us back with twelve years of increasing devotion. In the simple way in which we love those back who love us for who we are, we loved him back, too. And love him still. He lives always in the hearts of our children and ourselves.

I cried so hard the day he died, a crying out of many deep rivers. I cried for my father who had died the year before, losing a brave struggle against the cancer that finally ravaged him. I cried for loneliness, for my mother who was then learning to live alone in a house that once held six, then just two, and finally just herself. I cried for my younger brother who was fighting what we thought at the time was a winning battle against cancer, but who taught us that each day is tentative, a gift we cannot completely trust but must completely value. I cried for myself, too, I think – for all the things I hadn't done, hadn't been, and would never do or be.

These many years later, distanced from that day, I am somehow more aware not only of the losses, but of the strengths of life. Of the laughter that my father gave us with his corny jokes and belief in our own uniqueness. Of the strength that my mother gave by showering her love and wisdom onto her children and grandchildren. Of the grace of a brave brother who taught us the gratitude and joy that can be wrested out of each and every moment. Of the richness that a damaged dog brought into the life of a growing family.

Every Thanksgiving when I sit around the table with those I love, I know how fortunate I am despite that which is lost. Life does not come easily, yet there are gifts everywhere. In that long ago year of farewells, I learned that everything that hurts us helps us grow, if we have the courage to use it and the strength to remain kind.

And so we say farewell when we must. And keep alive within ourselves the gift of gratitude interwoven within the joys and the sorrows of this immensely complicated, immensely precious journey that is ours.

All Too Human

The movie "Lincoln," caused many people to turn fresh eyes to this 16th President of the United States. I have been, from childhood on, Lincoln-crazed. I'll never forget the first time I viewed the Lincoln Monument, staring up at his sculpted face on a rainy night in Washington, almost losing my breath at the beauty of it all. It is his sorrowful eyes, his profound words, his meaningful life. In the lines of Lincoln's face we see who he was, a simple man in complicated circumstances, a man trying to save a nation raging against itself, a man working to remain principled in times that were often unprincipled. And, instead of that historical context making him egotistical or grandiose or pompous, it made him more thoughtful, more patient, more human. He was someone all leaders should be. And we identify with him too because we also have faced hard times, have become lost in complicated places, have been in our own sorrowful deserts. He was there in the extreme, and he remained steadfast just the same. We like that about him.

I read once that the best leaders for difficult times are those who have suffered. It might be one of the keys to the puzzle of what made Lincoln great. The stereotype of Lincoln is one of his growing up in a loving, hard-working family in a log cabin in Illinois. And there is much truth to that image of happiness. Lincoln did have a very loving mother, Nancy Hanks, who taught Lincoln the values of love, honesty, and truth that would fore-shadow the man he was to become. Lincoln sometimes spoke of his "angel mother." Historians have wondered whether that statement was made about Nancy Hanks who died when Lincoln was 9 years old, the first great tragedy of his life, or about Sarah Bush Lincoln, who became Lincoln's second mother upon his father's remarriage. Sarah also adored Lincoln and once called him "the finest boy I ever knew" despite having her own biological sons.

Yet life is seldom accurately portrayed in simple images, and Lincoln's relationship with his father was much more difficult and fairly unhappy. For, while Abraham was a thoughtful boy who loved to spend his hours reading books and reflecting, his father Thomas was a man of his times who spent his days working the fields, fishing, and hunting, tasks Abraham disliked enormously. Out of necessity, Abraham did work the land with his father, but he would return to his books at every opportunity. Lincoln's father sometimes thought his son lazy and indolent. A cousin at the time recalled Lincoln's father once striking Abraham to the ground in anger. In adulthood, the relationship between Lincoln and his father was never completely repaired, and Lincoln did not come to his father on his deathbed, even after a request from Abraham's brother. "Say to him," Abraham wrote, "that if we could meet now, it is doubtful whether it would not be more painful than pleasant." As Ronald White writes in *A. Lincoln*, "The distance could not be bridged."

Yes, suffering was a shadow throughout Lincoln's life. The death of his son Eddie in Springfield, Illinois before he left for Washington, and later the death of Willie in the White House were unconquerable sorrows for Lincoln. And Lincoln seemed to sense the difficult days ahead when he left Springfield for Washington. "Here I have lived a quarter of a century and have passed from a young to an old man. Here my children have been born, and one is buried. I now leave, not knowing when, or whether ever, I may return with a task before me greater than that which rested upon Washington." His words ring with the sorrow of a man understanding the challenges to come.

In her incredible book, *Team of Rivals*, Doris Kearns Goodwin writes that Lincoln "possessed extraordinary empathy – the gift or curse of putting himself in the place of another, to experience what they were feeling, to understand their motives and desires...Lincoln's remarkable sense of empathy was inevitably a source of pain." And a contemporary of Lincoln's, Helen Nicolay, wrote of Lincoln, "With his sympathy, his conscience, and his unflinching sense of justice, he was predestined to sorrow."

Lincoln's empathy regarding the suffering he witnessed in slavery and on the fields of battle pained his soul throughout his lifetime. Despite the fact that revisionists sometimes argue that Lincoln never really was that opposed to the institution of slavery, his words from childhood on dispute those claims. Some of the many things Lincoln wrote and said demonstrated his passion on the issue. "If slavery is not wrong," he said, "then nothing is wrong." "Those who support the institution of slavery ought to try it on themselves." "Slavery is the eternal struggle between right and wrong throughout the world."

The slaves at the time knew of the president's abhorrence of slavery. When the war ended and Lincoln went south to survey the damage, former slaves lined the streets bowing their heads in homage to this man who had understood their suffering, who had suffered himself, and who had fought for their deliverance.

I am thinking of Lincoln a lot these days for many reasons. We live in a time of great political divisiveness, a time when civility is often all but absent from public dialogue and when spurious verbal attacks are common. It is no surprise that President Barack Obama is a great admirer of Lincoln, for they share many of the same characteristics and dilemmas: a divisive political climate; a character of measured calm and a finely-tuned sense of humor; a yearning for civil rights for all; and a desire to bring people together in understanding. Lincoln's words to a friend could speak for both of them. "I don't like that man," Lincoln once said. "I will have to get to know him better."

Each year, we commemorate Lincoln's birthday as a real gift of the heart. He was truly a simple person in complicated circumstances. And what we admire about him most, what we see in that face, is his ability to stay steady and firm and to do the right thing in the midst of great adversity and devastation. We look at him, and we see how, at certain points in our lives, we have been simple people in complicated circumstances that feel too great for us to manage. And yet sometimes, like Lincoln, we have been able to move forward with our finest motives. Sometimes, we have carried on with grace and hope through the hardest of times. Sometimes, in our most difficult heartaches, we muddle through the troubles, take a breath, and try to stay strong.

Like Lincoln, we never do it perfectly well, and we stumble a lot. But something in him is something in us as well. Imperfect, wounded, but trying just the same.

"With malice toward none, with charity for all."

Lincoln. A soul for all times.

The Top Cop

The tip of his thumb is shot off. His voice is raspy, and always will be, from the bullet that raced through his larynx and vocal cords. And as I talked to him, he pulled his blue shirt collar aside to show the scars that line his throat. He is Lieutenant Brian Murphy, and he was the very first responder at the Sikh Temple shooting of August 5, 2012 in Oak Creek, Wisconsin.

Brian was raised in a hard-working family, the son of a middle class sanitation worker. He was short in stature until his last year of high school, and he remembers being picked on. "Bullying, they would call it today," he said. Growing up, he was sometimes confused and sad. But he was set on becoming a police officer. It was what he always wanted to do.

The reader may remember Lt. Brian Murphy at the President's State of the Union Address, being recognized by President Barack Obama for his courage and his heroism. "That's just the way we are made," Obama quoted Murphy as saying when he asked him how he was able to do what he did.

I reminded Brian that he could have said, "That's just the way I am made," but he was intentional in his wording. "I'm not a hero," he will tell you. "Any of the officers I work with would have done the same thing in my place."

Perhaps, I think to myself. But, as I talked with Lieutenant Murphy at length, I realized that he is not just a hero for what he did, but for the role model he has provided after the traumatic event that left six people dead and four wounded. Being shot 15 times with 25 rounds and with two bullets still in him has changed Brian in profound ways. He talks often about the life lessons he brings from his experience.

"I knew I had to endure," he says of his time during and after the shooting. He talks of the role model his mother and his sister had been years before in fighting their cancer to the end, even after it was apparent that they would die of it. "In various ways," he said, "We all have to try to endure, and to come out stronger for it. I knew I needed to be as brave as they had been."

Although the aftereffects of the shooting led to Brian's retirement from his beloved police work, he was philosophical as he spoke of the "next chapter" of his life to come. He knew he needed to look forward, beyond his own tragedy to a larger vision. He speaks of how we all need to keep going. "The toughest guy in the room," he says, "is the one who gets out of bed every morning and goes to work."

Murphy is also changed by his interaction with the Sikh religion which he told me is the fifth largest religion in the world. "I couldn't believe how readily they forgave the shooter, the very same day. Their whole belief system is based in peace and kindness and love. I couldn't forgive as quickly as they did. They've taught me so much."

When asked about the shooter and the Skinhead and other hate groups, he is philosophical. "We need to create a mission of teaching love and removing ignorance. That must happen."

But the strongest part of Murphy's message is one that relates to all of us. For he understands that every person is wounded, hurt, broken in some way. And yet his message is for everyone. "Don't ever give up – it's too easy," he says. "The cloak of self-pity is warm, but it isn't too comfortable."

The most impressive part of his lesson, though, is the lesson of gratitude. "We don't always appreciate what life is until something like this happens to us. Afterwards, you realize how unimportant some of the things are that we worry about. Life is such a gift."

Is Murphy trying to change the world? He is certainly trying to make a difference for others and those to come after us. But his response is interesting when you ask him the greatest lessons he's learned.

"What we need to do is to show optimism in the face of hardship and to be relentless in working toward the betterment of oneself."

"Relentless in working toward the betterment of oneself." Words of a thoughtful man who understands that we make the world a better place when we make ourselves better people.

A simple lesson from a hero.

The betterment of oneself.

It is worth being relentless about.

Two New Years

I wrote the following on New Years Day in 1994, three days before my younger brother's surgery for cancer. And I was in the hospital waiting room in Madison those three days later when the doctors came from post-op to report of the tumor, "We got it all." We cried tears of joy, and my brother got twelve more years to spend with his family and friends before the cancer reappeared, more aggressive than before. He passed away in April of 2006 at the young age of 55. He was a man who lived his life understanding the value of joy, laughter, and gratitude, and he never became embittered or angry. In fact, in hospice a few days before his death, a friend shook his head and said to him, "You know, sometimes life just isn't fair." And my brother's response was immediate and gentle, "You know," he said, "I really don't feel that way." He knew the gifts of his life, and he felt he had been a lucky man. And so, these many years later, I share these words written when he was first diagnosed as we begin another year of this very brief and very precious journey with him in our hearts.

New Years Day, 1994 - This New Years is a different one for me. Only two days before Christmas, I learned that my younger brother has cancer, and that it is malignant. He will face surgery, chemotherapy, and the hardest of all questions. And those of us who love him are left to wonder if this isn't only a dream we will wake from.

Don has always been a light in our family. The youngest of four children – boy, girl, girl, boy – he was, from little on, the one who could make everyone laugh, the one who tuned into everyone's feelings, a gentle, sensitive peacemaker, and a great lover of people. He was the one whose blond hair and bright eyes lightened my childhood. He was the one I mothered like he was my own. He was the one who I trudged to the dime store with for "penny candy," the one who went trick-or-treating with me.

23

He was the one who won the marble games and made the yoyos work. He was the one who told jokes to the company. He was the one who brought a myriad of friends – and assorted pets – into our house. He was the one to marry his high school sweetheart and, within a family we all look up to, raise their four beautiful children.

Last week, he was the one to joke, as he was complimented on his slim build, his healthy eating habits, his active life, "Yes, at least I've got my health."

So now it seems only appropriate that he is the one assuring us, telling us that everything will be all right. And we have not words enough left in all the world to tell this gentle, special man what he has been to us and how much we love him. Our stammered ramblings are a paltry testament to the quality of his person. He is a prince among men, a gentle, understated, good, good man. And so we stand here speechless in the presence of his life.

Still this New Years, despite this pain, this shadow, I feel somehow certain that my brother will be all right. As my teenage son states so matter-of-factly, "Uncle Don's just too great a guy not to be okay." So I eagerly share my son's optimism, telling myself that the cancer will be contained, that we will share many future holidays and future memories carved from the everyday events of busy family lives.

And yet this New Years leaves me with more measured thoughts, with a new reality. I now know firsthand what so many sentimental movies and stories remind us of. We, each of us, are only promised the moment we are in right now – that, and nothing more. And so it is now, this year, that we must do what it is that we can do.

It is now that we must hug our children, heal old wounds, comfort ourselves, settle up accounts.

It is now that we must watch a snowstorm, tell a violet a very old secret, lean against a tree and do nothing but listen.

It is now that we must walk through large doors, enter great rooms, dream great dreams.

It is now that we must draw a picture, learn piano, make a collage, canoe down the river.

It is now that we must study the ants to learn how to build, watch a baby sleep to learn how to breathe, deep listen to someone over 80 to learn how to grow.

It is now that we must write a poem, or a book.

It is now that we must wear wide-brimmed hats and worn out shoes.

It is now that we must give gifts of the heart, take our parents hands and tell them what a legacy they have given us, thank our partner and our children and our family and our friends, for simply being there.

It is now that we must stand on a street corner and yell for all the world to hear, "Happy New Years to us."

It is now that we must realize that this is all that's promised us, this moment – and perhaps, if we are lucky – this year. Nothing more.

And it is now that we must realize just what a gift that is.

It is, After All, About Justice

*Unitarian Universalist Minister Rev. Dr. Tony
Larsen Leading the Vigil Group in Song*

*"Justice will come when those who are not injured are as
indignant as those who are."*
– Thucydides

Sacred Ground

Last week, we stood huddled together in the street on a frigid, dark night with a wind chill of twenty below. There were only a few of us at the beginning, but there were nearly a hundred by the vigil's end. We stood on that dark street where, a week before, a woman had been murdered.

The people at the vigil were diverse. Some were family members and friends of Jennifer and some were community members. The participants shared one common cause whether they came from nearby or further away. They came to stand together at a sacred site where a fellow citizen had spent the final hours of her life. They gathered together to affirm, with songs and with words, that we stand on holy ground when we stand where another's journey has ended.

The site where the shooting occurred was within yards of us. Some of those present knew the victim and some didn't, some were from the neighborhood and some were from farther away, some were senior citizens and some were children. The lyrics of one of the songs spoke to this diversity, "We are a land of many colors, and we are singing, singing for our lives. We are young and old together, and we are singing, singing for our lives. We are a gentle, loving people, and we are singing, singing for our lives..."

For many years now, when someone in our community dies in an act of violence, Rev. Tony Larsen of the Unitarian Universalist Church leads mourners and members of the community in candlelight vigils sponsored by the local Interfaith Coalition and held at the site of the incidents. Whether the vigils are for gang members or prominent citizens, young people or adults, little-known citizens or the well-known, a congregation of people gathers together in a tribute to the loss that has taken place and to the individual who is now gone. Some of the vigils, like this one, are large, and some are very small. But, whatever their size, their meaning is profound.

The details of the vigils vary, but what never changes is the pain of the loss. There is always someone to speak for the victim who died, and the many victims left in the wake of the tragedy. This time, people spoke of the victim's humor, her kindness, the good mother she was, and how much she would be missed. Others spoke of the need for forgiveness in our hearts. Some spoke for the need for peace and for an end to the violence that shakes our world.

We sing of that destruction, "I have a dream within my heart, I have a dream within my heart, and for a world that's come apart, I have a dream. I have a hope within my heart, I have a hope within my heart, and for a world that's come apart, I have a hope. I have a love within my heart, I have a love within my heart, and for a world that's come apart, I have a love…."

The candles held by the participants symbolize the reason for these ceremonies. Light has always represented the inner gifts which everyone has, the spark of imagination within, the humanity of all people. We hold a symbol of light, our vigil candles, as we sing again, "This little light of mine, I'm going to let it shine/All around Racine, I'm going to let it shine/All around Wisconsin, I'm going to let it shine/Let it shine, let it shine…"

Rev. Larsen speaks to the reason for these vigils. "We believe," he says, "that when someone dies, the community loses a part of itself and, since each life is sacred, we come to re-sanctify the ground and to be activists for peace in our lives. We leave here wearing our black ribbons as symbols of another loss. If people ask us why we have the ribbons on, we can tell them that our sister died, for we are all sisters, all brothers in this life, and we know that each and every death through violence is another death too many."

Jennifer's death was indeed a violent one. She was a victim of the abuse that finally killed her. Some people from the Women's Resource Center were present to highlight the importance of addressing abuse in our community and nation. Others asked for an end to gun violence, a current and recurring issue for our times, an issue that needs action now. All recognized the importance saying farewell at the end of Jennifer's journey. These vigils at the sites of the murders that occur far too often in our community are a way of marking another life gone, another journey completed, another legacy bestowed. We mourn and yet we also sing some songs of hope. "I believe in a miracle, oh yes I do, I believe in a miracle 'cause I believe in you. I believe we'll have peace someday, oh yes, I do. I believe we'll have peace someday 'cause I believe in you."

At the end of the vigil, we are asked to hug people that we don't know as a way of acknowledging the commonality of this human experience – that when one suffers, we all suffer, when one is in pain, we all are in pain, and when one of us dies, part of all of us dies.

No one really knows for sure what lies beyond this life we travel. What we do know is that our time here is precious, that each life has beauty and dignity, and that how we spend our moments matters. Those who stood clinging together in the frigid evening air with our flickering candles understood the message of this night. We were here to honor a fellow traveler and to acknowledge the humanity, the sadness, the forgiveness and, yes, the hope that is all part of the human condition. We need each other, and we know it.

And so, as fellow travelers, we will gather together at these vigils as often as we must in hopes of that time when we won't have to stand together for this reason anymore - in hopes of that time when we will know a more peaceful community, a more peaceful country, a more peaceful world. We will work toward that time and toward those laws that will make peace possible.

"We have a hope within our hearts, we have a hope within our hearts, for a world that's come apart, we have a hope........"

And it may yet come to be.

Just a Girl

"You're just a girl," the little boy taunted me on the grade school playground when I wanted to enter their game. "Girls don't play baseball," he said smugly as he strode away. Oddly, I don't remember feeling too hurt or sad. It was just the way things were back then, and we knew its truth from the times themselves. He was right, after all. I was "just a girl."

And I would be taught the truth of that phrase many times thereafter.

When I was in college, I remember scanning the newspaper classifieds for summer jobs, and the column headings that jumped out at me, "Help Wanted Male" and "Help Wanted Female." The "Help Wanted Male" column was full of worlds of opportunity...firefighters, salesmen, engineers, managers, lawyers, an endless list. The "Help Wanted Female" column had far fewer options, secretaries, nurses, clerical assistants, hairdressers. It was abundantly clear that there were only limited roles for women in the world of work.

It would not be accurate to compare the discrimination women faced in those years with the discrimination faced by racial minorities at the time. Women, at least, were protected from the worst of discrimination by the fact that there were at least some professional fields open to us. We did not face what many minorities did, the availability of only lower-paid work, the barriers to joining the ranks of the economically well-off, and the knowledge that their children, no matter what their academic success, would most likely not be among the working professionals of the world. The sheer unfairness of it all was breathtaking.

Still, women my age know the price of prejudice. When I graduated from a large public high school in a big city, I was among the top students in my class. I was a bookish girl, and the teachers respected my work and honored that by giving me the best college scholarship available to a girl, a fully-paid ride. I've never forgotten that, yet there are other things I've never forgotten either.

I've never forgotten that, about the time I was awarded that scholarship, I spoke with my high school counselor about career choices and told him that I wanted to go to medical school. I remember how strangely he looked at me before he said, in a kindly voice, "That is not a good field for a woman. What would you do if you wanted to get married?" This, from a high school counselor.

I've never forgotten that I babysat during the summer for the children of a doctor and his wife and that, when he was driving me home, I mentioned to him that I was thinking about applying for medical school after college. He, too, said that he didn't think I should do that since the women he knew in medical school ended up getting married and never using their degrees. "Those spaces in medical schools," he said, "could have gone to men who would have continued being in practice." Even back then, I doubted that many women would invest in all of the time and work of medical school and then never use their degree.

I've never forgotten the physics professor at UW-Madison who I went to talk to about a project only to be faced with an almost explosive rage when I raised the subject of applying for medical school. "Women don't belong in these fields," he admonished me. "Their brains and temperaments are just not suited to it." And he said this to me, a strong student in his physics class.

I remember my parents, too, and their tepid response to my plans to pursue medical school. They were wonderful parents who saw to it that their daughters as well as their sons went to college and sought careers. Still, their reaction to my goal left a lasting negative impression.

Be it blatant or subtle, prejudice is a slippery slope. In the end, the discouragement proved too much for me, a wall I couldn't climb over being who I was, raised as a nice girl at a time when marriage was the spoken and unspoken goal set for women. I wish I could go back and be stronger, and wiser, and braver. But the times we live in shape us beyond our imagining. There were women in those days, although not many, who pursued medical school, law school, the police academy, firefighting, and other of the myriad of then almost exclusively male careers. But the barriers were enormous.

Our oldest daughter is an MD, as is her husband. Oddly, I never shared my story with her, and was surprised when she came home from college one day to say that she was going to apply to medical school. I was stunned and pleased, taken aback by this sudden, unexpected career path. Now, after much work, she is a doctor and she has much to show for her choices.

Besides having a successful career that she loves, she is a wonderful mother to three children while balancing an amazing schedule. I watch her, and am very proud of both her doctoring and her parenting. And I note, with some irony, that her career balances perfectly with raising a family. She has flexibility in her schedule, the fulfillment of making a difference, and time to spend with her young family. I ponder how the counselors, the professors, the parents and the doctors themselves could have missed all of that possibility back in our growing up years.

I would never have used the "discrimination" word back then for what I experienced. Women were, after all, spoken of in the most generous of terms – we were the adored girlfriends, the beloved mothers, the gentle grandmothers of our time. Now I see, though, that even that was touched with discrimination, laced with prejudice, full of booby traps. A recent book spoke of the need for women to be afforded "care and protection" as if it is only women who need those things.

Once my husband took a seminar that his company offered on gender discrimination, and he was amazed by what he saw. Some women in that session cried, tears running down their faces, at the opportunities they had missed because of the barriers they faced. They talked of their brothers going to college when they and their sisters weren't sent because they "will just get married anyway." They spoke of being passed over for promotions that ultimately went to men simply because the men "had families to support." They talked about what they might have become if all avenues had been open to them.

Yes, as women we understand the toll that discrimination takes on individuals and generations. Society pays an enormous price for the talent it overlooks when doors are closed to some based on skin color, nationality, religion, gender, sexual orientation, handicaps, or any of the life situations that make individuals different from the norm.

"It isn't easy being green," Kermit wisely told us. Some of us know that from our life experience. And those who do need to tell our stories to our young girls and our young boys, not only to keep advancement alive, but to help them understand the larger issues of prejudice. If we don't tell them these stories, they may never really know how a person can be derailed from their dreams by external factors that have nothing to do with who they really are or what they can become.

Hopefully, the boy on the playground who told me that I was "just a girl" has daughters and granddaughters of his own now and sees possibilities abound for them. Hopefully, we have all learned from the past. As Helen Reddy's famous old song reminds us, "Yes, I am wise, but it's wisdom born of pain. Yes, I've paid the price, but look how much I've gained. If I have to, I can do anything."

For we women are not now, and never will again be, "just a girl."

Even When It Hurts

It seems that the controversy regarding book censorship and especially about which books should be banned from school library shelves will continue forever. While the breadth of the censorship has changed since ebooks and technology, there remain surprising books that still appear on lists of books to be removed from school libraries. Here are some of them.

"Of Mice and Men," by John Steinbeck; "The Chocolate War," by Robert Cormier; "The Catcher in the Rye," by J.D. Salinger; "The Adventures of Huckleberry Finn," by Mark Twain; "Deenie," by Judy Blume; "Go Ask Alice," author anonymous; "A Light in the Attic," by Shel Silverstein; "Forever," "Then Again Maybe I Won't," and "Blubber," all by Judy Blume; "To Kill a Mockingbird," by Harper Lee; "Cujo," by Stephen King; "The Diary of Anne Frank," by Anne Frank, and so many more.

Book censorship might have some validity if the books people objected to were trash. The shocking, eye-opening truth gleaned from the list above is that many books objected to are not trash, but books of incredible, redeeming, lasting value. They are books that make us smile, like "A Light in the Attic." They are books that make us afraid like "The Chocolate War." They are books that ask us to come face-to-face with our true feelings about differences like "To Kill a Mockingbird." They are books that echo generations of young people asking how they can grow up in a world that is so often phony, like "Catcher in the Rye." And they are books that speak of the enduring quality of the human spirit and what genuine depth of character is like "The Adventures of Huckleberry Finn." They are, essentially, books that speak to the truth of the human condition.

The danger of book censorship lies in its assumption that we must not delve into that which is different or unpleasant or troubling or aberrant among us. No more reading of youth struggling for identity, of the despair of the rootless, of the questioning of conventional values, or of the darkness and evil that can surface in the human spirit. No more reading about how badly we have sometimes failed as a people.

Someone once said, "I never met a bigot who was a reader as a child." The central value of fiction is that it opens our eyes in a way nothing else can. When we read fiction, we are allowed to step inside another person, to see life as someone else does, to become more sighted than we are.

That is why, so many years ago, the Puritans would not allow their members to read fiction, and it is why today, certain groups are so frightened of books that speak with clarity and vision to the depths of the human experience. There are those who need to see the world as black and white, good and evil, them versus us.

Books that shake us to our foundations, that ask us to search, are books of value. And those are the very books that the censors would take from our lives. Not trash, but stark honesty is what is really being objected to.

We must read that we might know. And we must continue reading, even when it hurts.

Turtles, Bumps, and Protests

In the years when my children were young and now that I have grandchildren, I have always loved reading them Dr. Seuss' parable about Yertle the Turtle, the tyrant king who preyed upon all of the lesser turtles of his realm. My young children and grandchildren would empathize with that poor little turtle named Mack groaning at the bottom of the stack of turtles which King Yertle had summoned to serve as his throne. And the kids were always glad when that plain little turtle named Mack "decided he'd taken enough. And he had. And that plain little Mack did a plain little thing. He burped! And his burp shook the throne of a king." From little on, I believe, some core place within us screams out against injustice in its many forms, rails against tyrants who view power as the ultimate goal, and understands that a greater battle is always taking place in these things. And so we cheer inwardly for little Mack and for all of the oppressed of this world.

One year, Time Magazine's chose "The Protestor" for their Person of the Year. That choice resonated with many since most of us have been, at one time or another, at the bottom of the stack, just like Mack, pressed down by forces acting with unfairness and injustice toward those at the bottom. If we haven't been there ourselves (and most of us have), we have certainly seen the scenario played out time and time again within our nation and throughout the world. And so we cheer when the oppressed finally prevail, as they ultimately always will.

The year of Time's Choice for "The Protestor" was a year of crying out for fairness. In Syria, in Jordan, in Egypt, in Spain, in Greece, in Chile, in Saudi Arabia, in India, in China, in the United States, and throughout the world, the protestors had taken to the streets. And nations came to realize the strength of those who demand rights and fairness and justice.

Ultimately, those forces do finally win out and the arc of history does bend toward justice.

The truth of this has been demonstrated time and time again and the oppressors could learn some lessons here. They could remember little Rosa Parks and how a civil rights movement exploded with her refusal to give up her seat. They could remember the lessons of Gandhi and how a simple man with a nonviolent march changed the future. They could remember the Boston patriots who protested the lack of representative government and about the democratic nation that grew out of that movement. They could remember the college students of the 1960s and the protests that led to the end of an unjust war, and the beginning of greater rights for minorities and women. They could remember the good Dutch people who erupted in a general strike in 1941 in protest of the actions the Nazis were taking against the Jewish people. They could remember the long struggle of Susan B. Anthony and the suffragists who were jailed and tortured for fighting for justice for women and who ultimately won the vote. They could remember Stonewall and the growing rights for gays and lesbians that resulted from this unfair attack against peaceful people. They could remember Nelson Mandela and the end of apartheid largely due to the courage of this man who spent years in prison for his efforts. They could remember the story of a Jewish carpenter who by embracing all people began a worldwide religion based on the love, understanding and tolerance of everyone, things many modern day Christians neglect to model.

The lists are endless...the tireless courage of Martin Luther King, the strength of Henry David Thoreau, the bravery of Jane Addams, the resoluteness of the protestors of Tiananmen Square, and the ongoing legions of those who speak truth to power. It could be said of them that which was written by Time Magazine of "The Protestors," "They dissented, they demanded, they did not despair even when the answers came back in a cloud of tear gas or a hail of bullets."

Time Magazine's decision to select a composite of "The Protestor" as their Person of the Year reflected solid wisdom. It served to remind those at the top that there are forces below that can be mighty indeed. It could remind those on the bottom that they actually have far more strength than they realize if they are just brave enough to use it. And it could ultimately lead to the kind of change that Dr. Seuss understood so well those many years ago when he wrote, "And the turtles, of course, all the turtles are free, as turtles and, maybe, all creatures should be."

And so to "The Protestor" worldwide, we say this. Over all of the years, you have made the world freer and fairer and more just. So, carry on. Be brave. Be strong. There are barriers to be broken still. And you can do it. We tip our hats to you and to the you within all of us, the Person of the Year, The Protestor.

Where would we be without you?

February, Love, and Laws

It is time that we all get used to it, for it is one of the last civil rights not to be fully addressed in our nation. It is time that we learn that people love who they love and that no one's love is more or less important than anyone else's. It is time that we learn that nobody's love merits greater or fewer rights than anyone else's. It is time that we learn.

As with most matters of truth and of the heart, it turns out that young people are usually the first ones to understand these lessons. Ask most young people if gays and lesbians should be allowed to marry and their response is strong and logical and direct, "Of course. Why not? Who are they hurting?" There are other answers to that question, though. There is the joke about the cynical response of a married heterosexual, "Sure. Why shouldn't they suffer like the rest of us?" And there is the dogmatic response of those who are fearful. "No, because homosexuality is an abomination."

Of course, the discussion about gay marriage should not center around humor or religion or even logic. The discussion should center around rights. And if we haven't learned that truth from slavery, or from the suffrage movement, or from the women's movement, or from disability laws, or from any of the civil rights initiatives, then we haven't been paying enough attention. For history has shown that it is our country, our democracy, our freedom that suffer when we withhold rights from any group of individuals.

Most people don't really know about what happened at the Stonewall Inn in New York in 1969 even though some of us were around at the time. Back then, no one talked about homosexuality much less about the rights of that community. Maybe that is why so few people have heard this story from our own American history. But it happened, and it is another saga of the pain we cause our nation and ourselves when we inflict unfairness and cruelty upon others.

It was June 28 of 1969 and many individuals were congregated at a bar in New York, the Stonewall Inn. The interesting thing about this event is that those in the bar were doing nothing other than drinking and conversing and spending a regular evening together. Suddenly, the police entered and raided the premises. In the 1960s, police raids on bars that were deemed gay and the persecution of sexual minorities was routine procedure. This time however, rather than going quietly to jail as had happened in so many places and times prior, the gay patrons resisted. Like Rosa Parks on the bus on that fate-altering day, they had had enough and they weren't going to take it anymore. They fought back and within days their protests became an activist cause that marked the beginning of the gay rights movement in the United States and around the world.

An irony in the long struggle for rights in our country is that, once a particular struggle proves largely successful, few can see the logic of those who fought against those rights. Within a few years, people realize that, of course we shouldn't have slavery. Of course, women should have the right to vote. Of course, we shouldn't have segregated facilities. And increasingly, we are hearing the refrain in a growing number of states and among so many young people, "Of course, gays should be allowed to marry. It doesn't hurt anyone." That day is right around the corner.

At the time of this writing, more and more states have legalized gay marriages, and that number will continue to increase as the rights of individuals override fear and the status quo. And the future will not label these relationships as civil unions or domestic partnerships, but as marriage. For this is a right called marriage equality, and its time has come. As Republican Representative Maureen Walsh stated in a hearing on the subject, "Yes, it is about equality. And why in the world would we not allow these equal rights for individuals who truly are committed to one another in life to be able to show that by way of marriage?" It is a great question. Maureen Walsh also noted that the role of those making laws is often to support the rights of the minority against a vocal majority. That is the American basic precept of our country, protecting the rights of all.

A number of years ago, the J.C. Penney Company announced that their spokesperson would be Ellen DeGeneres, a popular and openly lesbian television host. A group called The Million Moms objected immediately because of her lack of "traditional values" and asked that Penneys reverse itself. The Company held its ground, and numerous consumers pledged to shop at JC Penneys because of its courage in standing up to bigotry. Ellen Degeneres stated that "my haters were my motivators," and she listed her values - honesty, equality, kindness, compassion, treating people the way you want to be treated, and helping other people. It sounded pretty much like traditional values to most of us. In the long run, fairness and common sense do ultimately rule the day.

We all make choices regarding what side of history we want to be on. We do that by the way we act, by what we say, by how we vote, and especially by what we do. This is a pivotal period in our country for the rights of the gay and lesbian community. We would all do well to ask ourselves, "When our descendants look back on us, would we have wanted them to see us as those who supported slavery? Would we have wanted them to see us as those who didn't think women should vote or have equal opportunities? And now, would we want them to see us as those who didn't think LGBT individuals should be allowed to marry or to enjoy the rights of all of the citizens of our nation?"

There is a phrase about the wisdom of "standing on the side of love." As this issue is debated, these would be good questions for each of us to ask ourselves. Do we believe in rights for all as our foreparents did? Do we recognize the worth and dignity of every individual? Ultimately, do we believe in our constitution or don't we?

And do we want history to record that we were among those individuals brave enough to remain standing on the side of love?

Our Home

"This is Not Good," the newspaper headline warned this week. And the article itself was even more alarming. It reported that in a recent month, national temperature records in the United States "weren't just broken, they were deep-fried." At least 7,775 weather stations across the nation reported breaking daily all-time high temperature records for the month of March. Climate scientists are worried. We all should be.

Each year in April, Earth Day is celebrated across the nation. For all of us, Earth Day should matter a great deal. It should matter because this celebration had its beginnings in 1969 under the leadership of Senator Gaylord Nelson who was concerned that green issues were not included on our national agenda. And, while the day had modest beginnings, it is estimated that in recent years, one billion people annually around the globe take part in Earth Day activities. That's an amazing statement about the devotion people feel globally toward this earth of ours.

Earth Day should matter a great deal to us because of our abundance of sparkling lakes, flowing rivers, nourishing fields, breathtaking hills and bluffs, and our incredible seasons that burst in a panorama all around us.

And Earth Day should matter a great deal to us because, truth be told, we know ourselves better through the gift of earth's waters, its air, and its green growing things. How many of us have not learned something of who we are while walking in a quiet lonesome woods, or looking down from one of the state's scenic bluffs and hills, or hearing the quiet lapping of the waves of one of our Wisconsin lakes? We are strangely connected to this earth, our home. We know it in our souls.

Recently, I read an article about global weather changes. It was not a political article. The author noted quite simply that we humans have become the major source of impact on the earth, so much so that some scientists call earth "the humanosphere." What we do has an impact. Not all of it is good.

Often now when we read about climate change and the environment, it is in a political context, a kind of them-versus-us analysis. And I am always amazed by this polarization since the earth and its future is so intrinsically interwoven with our own futures and the futures of our children. Whatever our political alignment, we should all care about the earth. There was a time when thoughtful people on both sides of the political aisle were united in their belief that we – all of us – have a deep, spiritual responsibility to take care of, to protect, and to honor this earth.

New information points to problems to come for our earthly home. Recent years have had the warmest weather temperatures in recorded history. The polar ice cap is melting at an alarming rate, enough to pose an enormous threat to animal and human life if allowed to continue unchecked. Seventy percent of the world's coral reefs are dead or dying. Storm intensities have more than doubled in the last thirty years. And the scientific community is almost unanimous in saying that the burning of fossil fuels, if continued, will have a devastating effect on the planet.

In the last few years, weather has been in the news constantly, and one can't help but believe that we humans are causing much of the turbulence. Is the heating of the globe causing the frequent fires, hurricanes, tornados, the droughts, the earthquakes, the tsunamis, the windstorms, the snowstorms, and more? Is our human activity causing this devastation? Are we the creators of our own tragedies?

I am thinking of all of this during this week of Earth Day, this week of bearing witness to both the breathtaking beauty around us and to our awesome responsibility for this earthly home of ours.

In time to come, others will breathe their first morning air standing where all of us once stood. And they will hopefully view the same seasonal panorama that fills us up. The bright birds of summer alighting on the branches. The autumn woods ablaze in golds and oranges and reds and purples. The winter crystalline chiming of the icy coating on the frozen trees. And they will hopefully also feel what we feel now, this exuberant bursting of springtime buds and flowers and birds, and of ourselves. "Now the ears of my ears awake, now the eyes of my eyes are opened," ee cummings wrote of spring.

Yes, how we treat the earth now for those yet to come matters a great deal indeed. The Native Americans said it best, "We do not inherit the earth from our ancestors. We borrow it from our children." They understood inherently that the gifts of the land and the water and the air are never really about ownership, but they are always about stewardship.

For today, I am blessed to be here, and I know it. So I think I'll take a woods walk now. And, as I walk, I will remember that it is up to each of us to be caring stewards of this earth of ours, and to be advocates for those things that might, even at this late date, save this earth, this place we call home.

We neglect that at our own peril.

Lethal

He was put to death in 2011 by lethal injection, and others await the same fate. Who knows if he was really guilty of the violent murder he was convicted of those 22 years ago?

Who knows?

In all of the pros and cons and all of the heated debate over the death penalty, it is those two words that should, in my mind, unsettle us.

Who knows?

Troy Davis was convicted on the eyewitness account of nine people, seven of whom later recanted their stories. The eyewitnesses say that they were threatened with jail for being accessory to the crime if they did not testify to Troy's guilt, something denied by the prosecution. Yet weakened by coercion and their own life circumstances, the eyewitnesses were not as strong as they should have been. They caved under the pressure as those in powerless situations so often do. And now Troy is, like the officer he swore he did not kill, also dead. He proclaimed his innocence to the end. He claimed that he had left the scene before any shots had been fired.

Who knows?

Some of the witnesses who recanted their first account implicated one of the original prosecution witnesses in the crime. The fact that there were three individuals who stated that the witness had confessed to them that he had committed the crime ultimately did not change anything.

Troy Davis was born October 9, 1968 in Butts County, Georgia and was put to death September 21, 2011 at the age of 42. Like so many who are on death row, he was a minority with a mixed history. He was the oldest child of Korean War veteran Joseph Davis, and his parents divorced while he was young. He grew up in Savannah, Georgia along with his four siblings. He was a poor student and dropped out of school in his junior year so he could get his younger disabled sister to rehab. Davis later received a GED in 1987. In 1988, he pled guilty to carrying a concealed weapon and was fined $250. Later that same year, Troy got a job as a drill technician at a manufacturing plant where he was considered likeable and a good worker until he stopped coming to work in December of that year. Davis later signed up for service in the US Marine Corps prior to the incident that Troy was arrested for and ultimately convicted of.

Davis had been scheduled to be put to death for the crime three times previous to September 21, 2011. He was scheduled for death on July of 2007, September of 2008, and October of 2008. Each execution was stayed. The execution of September 21, 2011 was not.

Almost a million people signed petitions urging the Georgia Board of Pardons and Paroles to grant clemency, among them Archbishop Desmond Tutu, Former President Jimmy Carter, Pope Benedict XVI, Former FBI Director and Judge William Sessions, Amnesty International, NAACP and numerous other individuals and organizations. The Board denied clemency and refused to reconsider its decision. There was a last minute appeal to the US Supreme Court but that was also denied, and Troy Davis was put to death.

Was this justice?

Who knows?

Legal experts have reported that the Antiterrorism and Effective Death Penalty Act of 1996 which was passed after the Oklahoma City bombing was a major obstacle in Davis' inability to get a new trial. The Act prohibits death row inmates from later presenting evidence they could have presented at trial. This ruling has been criticized by attorneys as restricting the rights of those wrongfully convicted to prove their innocence.

I do not support the death penalty. It seems to me that if we believe that murder is wrong, then it is wrong for the state and nation, too. And almost every major industrialized nation in the world with the exception of the U.S. has outlawed the death penalty. Still, most people in the U.S. support it. In a Gallup Poll taken in October of 2009, 65% supported the death penalty for those convicted of murder. In the same Gallup Poll question in 1965, only 45% of those polled supported the death penalty. It is one of those startling

statistics that should be considered by all of us when there is discussion regarding what has happened to the soul of America.

A newscaster recently said that, if the state is going to continue killing
people using the death penalty, then the law should be not "beyond a reasonable doubt," but "beyond any doubt." Indeed, for anyone who cares about
justice, it is what we should want. For there is one thing all justice-seeking
people do know. If the state takes a human life for alleged reasons of justice,
then it had better be absolutely positive that it has the right person, absolutely positive that it has the actual perpetrator.

Maybe Troy Davis committed the murder and maybe he didn't. Maybe
the state murdered the right man, and maybe it didn't.

Who knows?

The state doesn't.

And it should.

Speaking Up

"Please remove your underwear," the gym teacher said as the photographer stood behind the camera." I was 18 years old and in a line of freshmen women at UW-Madison. It was the late 60's and Physical Education was a required course. As part of the semester curriculum, we were required to have nude photos taken of each of us at the beginning of the year.

"Face front," the photographer said. And, a minute later, "Now, turn sideways."

When the ordeal was over, we walked out and put our underwear back on, humiliated, embarrassed and silent. The Phy Ed teacher said these were "posture pictures." Despite that, in my class at least, no other mention was made of posture for the rest of the semester.

On the rare occasions when I tell this story, something I never did until recently, people are either aghast or they simply don't believe it. "Go online and find the articles," I told some friends recently. "It really happened. And it happened for years." At UW-Madison, the photos were only taken of the girls, not the boys. I guess the boys had better posture!

About ten years ago, my sister told me that she had nude photos taken in gym class at UW-Madison and, surprised, I told her I had also. She is three years older than me, and seemed amazed, "They still took those pictures three years later!" I think on some level, we thought it was just our own classes since no one spoke of it.

A decade or so ago, I came across an article about this UW-Madison practice and I finally began to talk about it. And I recently went online to try to determine how long this was done. To my amazement, I found an article about this being common in the large, prestigious schools out east. That article didn't even mention the University of Wisconsin. And the procedure went on for years, from the 1930s to the 1960s.

The universities say that these photos have long since been destroyed, although there is an urban legend that some fraternities in Madison obtained access to the pictures and had a field day. The truth of that has never been verified.

It turns out, according to the article, that my sister and I are in famous company. Diane Sawyer and Hillary Clinton are among the parade of women who were photographed in the nude freshman year by their university Physical Education Departments. Looking back, the overriding questions loom large. Why didn't we speak up? Why didn't we tell anyone? And what were these universities thinking?

One reason we didn't talk was simply age. We were naive, young students, freshmen, away at a big university for the first time. On some level, we must have believed that this is just what happens to freshmen girls.

Another reason was simple embarrassment. Can you imagine the answer you'd give to the common parental question, "How was school today?" "Oh, mom, we just had our nude photos taken." It was nothing you wanted to talk about.

Finally, it was a little before the time of Viet Nam, before those years when we learned to question so many things, when on some level we lost trust, when we learned that institutions don't always get it right. An older woman is quoted as saying about the photos, "It was something you had to do. You didn't question it." And a blogger who asked her aunt about the photos heard much the same thing. "It was a different time," her aunt said, "You didn't question authority in the way you would now."

People often believe that they are not affected by the mores and culture of their times, that they can be independent of all of that. And there certainly is a spectrum of independent thinking among people. But there is a lesson here as well. This photography issue ended sometime before 1970. Until then, masses of women went silent about a practice that would have ended much sooner if we had spoken out.

And so it is now also, and about even more important issues. Our voices make a difference. The easiest thing to do in controversy is to stay silent about the wrongs of the world and to go about as if they aren't happening.

It's a good way to stay out of trouble and remain in calm waters. Yet that choice makes the waters more turbulent for those to come after us.

So from climate concerns to educational funding to gun control to any of a myriad of issues, it is always better when we speak out.

Things change when voices are raised, and the arc of justice inches slightly forward with each voice that is heard.

That is the story of history. That is the story of progress.

Things can change. Or be changed. If we just speak up.

It is up to us.

Courage

I have been thinking a lot these days about grief and suffering and courage. I have been pondering how people move forward from dark places, and why they do. So perhaps it was prophetic that I ended up interviewing a holocaust survivor for my radio program. The same questions I have been asking myself rose to the surface when I met her. Questions about her grief, her suffering, and her courage.

Raye is a diminutive 84-year old woman peering out from clear eyes, seemingly surveying her surroundings with unusual acuity. "We always had to be on the alert," she stated. "We had to watch out for everything all of the time," this holocaust survivor told me. It may explain the watchfulness of her demeanor on the day of the taping.

Raye was fifteen when she was in the first of four concentration camps in which she lived, although she told them that she was seventeen so that they would see her as able to work. At one point, Raye was in the Bergen-Belsen camp where Anne Frank died.

"Did you know her?," I naively inquired.

"Maybe," she replied. "Maybe she worked right next to me. We didn't talk too much. We didn't know each other. My mother, my aunt, and I were in all of the camps together, but we stayed away from each other and used different last names. They tried to separate families," she explained.

Raye has many stories to tell.

She tells of her aunt, her mother's sister, whose beautiful four-year old daughter was snatched away from her by the Nazis as the aunt screamed and begged and wept. Raye herself still cries every time she thinks of her little cousin. "How could adult human beings, maybe with children of their own, do such a thing?," she agonizes. Years later, Raye learned that those children were all put on train cars and taken to be exterminated.

She tells of the emaciated bodies walking around like skeletons. "We were all hungry all of the time," she stated matter-of-factly. She tells of being beaten to within an inch of her life for stealing a potato.

She tells of being ordered to dig holes in the ground for hour upon hour only to be told to fill them up again and dig new ones right next to them.

She tells of truckloads of dead bodies.

The holocaust haunts so many, as it has haunted me since youth. Maybe because I had a skinny, prematurely gray 8th grade teacher who survived the concentration camps and, while he seldom spoke of it, he carried always a sorrow-laden look in his eyes. Maybe because *The Diary of Anne Frank* was one of the earliest books that made me a reader and because I always remember Anne's hope, "Despite everything, I still believe that people are good at heart." Maybe because a friend of ours was a holocaust survivor who lost his entire 4th grade class in Poland to extermination in the camps after he and his family narrowly escaped to the U.S. Maybe because the overriding questions of the holocaust are so daunting. How could those things have happened? Could it have been stopped sooner? How did Hitler become who he was? How did so many people go along with the atrocities? And, the most difficult question of all, what is the nature of humankind to be able to do such things and where would we have stood in the midst of such tragedy?

The new year is an important time to reflect on the story of Raye and the legion of others who saw too much, suffered too much, and lost too much. As I ponder grief and suffering and courage, I find great lessons in Raye's words, perhaps three foremost.

"I do not hate," Raye proclaims. "If I hated, then Hitler would have won." She says it proudly and often, and it is reminiscent of some beloved words of Martin Luther King, Jr. "Let no one pull you so low as to make you hate them." Would that nations and peoples could adopt such a vision of peace for the years to come.

Secondly, Raye reminds us of the importance of telling our stories. Raye goes to schools and to civic groups and to radio programs to talk of her holocaust experiences. "Why do you do that?," I asked her, and she responded with passion. "Because we must never forget these things," she says. "Because people must know what happened for it not to happen again." It is much like Eisenhower said when he visited the concentration camps, "The things I saw beggar descriptions...the visual evidence and the verbal testimony of starvation, cruelty and bestiality were so overpowering. I made the visit deliberately in order to be in a position to give first-hand evidence of these things if ever in the future there develops a tendency to charge these allegations to propaganda."

We too have stories, not as tragic perhaps as Raye's story, but important just the same. We have stories of wars, the great depression, civil rights, women's rights, September 11, Katrina and so much more. We too can tell the truths of our times to our young people so that they know as reality the story of history, good and bad. We too can bear witness.

Finally, from Raye's story we see not only grief and pain, but courage and choice. For all that she endured, Raye could have chosen to bury herself in sadness, to become bitter, or to close doors on the possibilities that could still lie ahead. Instead, she chose life. "I have had a good life," she pronounces with words that ring with irony. She tell of her dear parents, her three children, her grandchildren. "Yes," she repeats as if wanting to be certain that the listener had heard her correctly. "I have had a good life."

It is a strange but important lesson as we look to the years ahead. We are all wounded in some ways, damaged by the death of loved ones or by abuse or the pain of war or loss of friendship or isolation or our own shortcomings, or a multitude of other wounds. So how do we survive? How did Raye? Can her life inform our own as we move forward?

Raye's story tells us that we can choose how we handle our wounds and our tragedies. There is a philosophy called choice theory that is empowering. It suggests that, while we often cannot choose what happens to us, we can choose what we do with those happenings. I was reminded of that philosophy by a sign I saw in a shop. "You cannot change the direction of the wind," it said, "but you can change the direction of your own sails."

And so in the years to come, as we consider the direction of our own sails, we can reflect on the words of courage, of choice, and of love to be gleaned from this 84-year-old holocaust survivor.

It is a new year.

Take heart.

Memories

Three of author's many uncles and aunts, circa 1905

"In many ways, we are not different than those who came before or those who come after us. We are human beings, seeking the light, searching for reason, asking continually what it is all about. And, in the midst of it all, we simply proceed, doing the best we can surrounded by Life, that great unfathomable mystery."
— Author's Journal Entry

Loss

One fall, many years ago, my son's second grade teacher transferred to a different school after two months into the school year. She was a sweet and dynamic individual who brought out the best in her students, and my son was heartbroken. I tried to explain to him about people reaching out for new challenges, about how she had been given a chance to try something she had wanted to do all her life, work with special needs students. I tried to talk with him about dreams.

My son wasn't able to fully grasp what I was saying, yet I sensed that he knew that this was something she must do. I sensed that he, too, understood a little of dreaming.

While that didn't make it any easier for him, it was perhaps his first experience with a truth he would experience many times thereafter. Sometimes we have to get out of the way for someone else. Sometimes we have to let go. Sometimes we have to hurt in order that those we love may make their own journey.

On the day of the going-away party for my son's teacher, I arrived early to help with the celebration. The decision to change pathways had not been arrived at easily by the teacher, and her reddened eyes gave testimony to the strain of the day and its partings.

Upon my entering the room, she walked over to me with a folded note in her hand. "I want to show you the note that Jeff gave me this morning."

I unfolded the paper and read his simple second grade words. "Don't feel so sad. You are in my heart. Love, Jeff."

A pile of gifts sat on the table, my son's among them, but I would guess that of everything received that day, this gift of words was perhaps the most treasured of all.

A week after the teacher had left, I was sitting on our family room couch with my son, both of us eating popcorn and watching a home video show. Out of solitary depths and with no connection to anything happening came the stillness of his voice.

"I miss her so much."

Although usually quick to comfort my children, I was silent this time. Only my hand over his told him that I understood. In loss, there is nothing to say, no words that are enough to soothe. And so my son had learned a second truth that he would learn many times over, and in much more difficult ways, too.

The sadness never really goes away, even when you've done the only thing you could have, even when you have let go.

In loss, there are not words enough to explain.

The Cardinal Alone

Looking out my kitchen window today, I watched the first cardinal I have seen in awhile, bright red and braving the winds of spring to peck at the frozen seed that had fallen from the bird feeder. Always when I see cardinals, the mate is nearby, watching and waiting, I'm never sure for what, but there all the same. Today, this bright red cardinal is alone.

I remember the years when my mother was living alone, too, after years of sharing life and its accompanying ups and downs with my father and, while we were there, the cacophony of children. Even after their children grew up and left, my mom and dad had each other and became recommitted to what had been their original roles before the advent of children and of life in high gear. Their quiet companionship in those times was a reminder of the continuity of it all and of the wholeness of a commitment that most people make when they are too young to comprehend its depth. Young and in love, they plunge into a lifetime. And, somehow during the process a steady wholeness takes hold. Yet the price of that union is that, toward the end, one must end up alone and survive in solitude the heavy quiet that comes after years of so much fuss and activity.

Periodically, our adult kids, their spouses, and our grandkids are home again, filling the house as everyone surrounds the dinner table with the abundance of food and commotion. I remember the many years when it was the two of us and our four children under one roof all of the time, with the kids bringing people in and out, some of whom I didn't even know. I remember a day when one of my son's friends asked him, "How many brothers and sisters do you have anyway?"

The assemblage of everyone again when it does happen is always chaotic. The kids arrive, the suitcases are brought in for those at a distance, and the toys are resurrected from the basement boxes marked, "Save for the grand-kids" before we even had grandkids. And the household chaos continues until the departure. Rather than wish for peace and order, I enjoy the commotion, knowing that soon enough the house will be quieter and I will again have my time to read and write and do those other things that also fill my life.

We raise kids to leave us, and we hope that each one of them, in their due time, will move anxiously and positively into the futures they create. It is an important part of the scheme of things. The next part, the spouses back together again remembering why they are partners, joined by their shared offspring and memories, is a healing part. But the hardest part, the part my mom endured, is the role that is more painful to accept, the losing of a companion, the stepping back into singleness again, the quietness of the days. On one of those long-ago days of my greatest household crazyness, my mother provided what I think of as the best advice she ever gave me. Enjoy this time. It goes so fast.

And so I enjoy deliciously the days when the chaos and noise occurs again, when there are once again too many people, young and old, in the house, and when the washing machine never stops. There is a beauty to each season, and the sound of these days will reverberate through the quieter springs to come, through the solitary roles that arrive later on.

Perhaps the cardinal, alone in the wind, has learned that lesson, too.

Monsters, Munchkins, and Memories

It is trick or treat day today, and lots of little urchins, monsters, witches and ghosts will arrive at our door, just as we did in those long ago days when we were the ones in costume. It reminds me how much life is the same from one generation to the next.

When I was little, trick or treat was always at night in the dark which made it extra scary. Back in those days, people didn't worry too much about safety issues. It was a time of people leaving their doors unlocked and trusting in the purity of the candy their children collected. It was also a time of nobody worrying much about what the sugar in the candy would do to their children. My parents just let us hoard our bags for as long as it took for us to eat it or tire of it. It was usually the latter, with much of our candy still there at Christmas, forgotten at the back of our closets. My parents seemed to sense that sometimes in life, going lightly and letting an event exist just for the fun of it was okay. It didn't seem to hurt us any.

When our kids were young, I took that same route my parents had those many years ago, and let the kids have their candy to look at, eat, count, trade, sort, and treasure. It seemed a tradition that served us well and I remember all the Halloween evenings that the kids counted and traded their candy, and the fun that they had.

There are some who worry about the ritual and the candy....too much sugar is bad for kids....ruins their teeth....causes bad behavior. Maybe. But today I heard a news report stating that numerous studies have confirmed that, despite what parents think, sugar does not have a negative impact on kids behavior. And, as far as the teeth thing, I've heard some dentists say that they'd rather the kids just get the candy, eat it, and get it over with in this once-a-year ritual.

I remember one Halloween when I was young and my little brother was sick in bed and about to miss out on trick-or-treating, a yearly highlight of our pretty much uneventful lives. He was so sad, and I was so sad for him. I walked far that night in the dark and asked for extra candy for my sick brother. Maybe some people thought that was a ploy, but it was a more trusting time back then and people, for the most part, believed me. I remember making a haul that night, and coming home to split the candy between the two of us. It was never really about the candy anyway as much as the ritual, the fun, the trading.

There are people who don't let their children celebrate Halloween because it is about witches and ghosts and goblins and graveyards or because it is scary or non-religious. But I can't resist thinking about the fun and lightness that those children miss. And there's a bigger issue here, too.

In life and in parenting, we always walk a fine line between following a tight and structured path or taking a path that winds and weaves a little, that allows for a little softness and a little less worry. In most things, especially regarding children, the second way was always the best for me. I was raised by gentle parents, and I believed so much in the goodness of children that I had no way to go but gentleness.

I remember a Literature class discussion about the Romanticists who believed children are born good and that civilization corrupts their innate goodness, versus the Classicists who believed that children are born with original sin and that they must be civilized by schools, churches, and institutions. Having held my little ones in my arms and having watched them grow in profound ways, I never could accept the second belief. Children trust us, and our job is to teach them, learn from them, and love them. Grandparents who oversee children the second time around understand that truth and the miracle of it all.

There is a Sandburg poem I read as a teenager about what advice a father should give to his growing son. He wrote, *"A father sees his son nearing manhood. What shall he tell that son? Shall he say, 'Life is hard. Be steel. Be rock.' This might serve him and guide him among sudden betrayals and tighten him for slack moments. Or should he say, 'Life is soft loam, be gentle, go easy.' This too might serve him. Brutes have been gentled where lashes failed. The growth of a frail flower on a path has sometimes up and shattered rock. A tough will counts. But so does desire. So does a rich, soft wanting. Without rich wanting nothing arrives."*

So maybe a little softness and levity helps children grow up to be thought-ful people (as stressful as that is), to be feeling people (as painful as that is), and to be loving people (as ache-filled and joy-filled as that is).

As the trick-or-treaters appear at my door, I hold out the bowl and let them choose their candies. "Thank you," they always say, somewhat shyly.

Happy Halloween, Monsters and Munchkins. Happy Halloween.

Where Would We Be Without Love?

February is indeed the month of love, a time to reflect on where we've been and where we are now.

I remember the first time I fell in love. I was nine years old and in fifth grade. His name was Michael. He had dark hair, almost black, and shockingly bright blue eyes. Freckles sprinkled across his face and even as a young boy, he was a devil-may-care kind of guy with a mix of sweetness, too. A sort of Rhett Butler before his time.

The teachers sometimes struggled with Michael and they would periodically call him up to stand against the wall, or to write repeating sentences on the board, or to stay in for recess to empty school wastebaskets. He was an unlikely candidate for my first love, especially because of the quiet, shy girl I was. But there was something about him. When he smiled at me, his heart was in his eyes and his gentle warmth was as clear as the sunshine on the first day of spring.

Valentine's Day at our elementary school was a banner day. We would spend hours at home decorating old shoe boxes with cut out cupids or candy hearts or construction paper in preparation for that special day. In our school, students could bring money to purchase valentines that cost anywhere from a penny up to 25 cents for the fancy ones. Of course, almost no one purchased the expensive valentines in this middle class neighborhood where pennies mattered and could be used at the dime store to purchase precious penny candy. The Valentines at our school were actually only elaborate holy cards or medals, but we didn't notice that oddity as we looked at their heart-shaped camouflage.

70

I remember my surprise on Valentine's Day that year at opening the cards in my shoebox and finding one of the expensive, big, red hearts edged with lace addressed to me. It was from Michael. My shy heart beat a little faster that day.

Of course, it was only puppy love. But with that early love comes that first heartthrob, that early recognition of the magic in someone else and in yourself, that serendipitous surprise of life changing suddenly.

Years later, I learned that Michael's mother had been an alcoholic, and that his home life had been far from ideal. That explained much about him, I thought all that time later. Children of alcoholics are often like Michael, gently seeking love that is elusive to them, noticing every change in a person's mood or temperament, looking to others for approval they can get only inconsistently at best in their own lives.

There is a part of me that misses Michael still. I lost touch with him when we went to different schools a year later, but I heard that he died young, in his 20s, while piloting an airplane. I thought of his daring as a little boy, the daring that would be reflected in his career choice of being a pilot. To this day, I hope his spirit soared as he flew through the air surveying the landscape below. Fly, Michael, fly.

Adolescence and young adulthood are probably the hardest part of the journey of romance for most people. It brings with it the opposing realities of the sudden ecstasy of joy and the crushing heartbreak of romance. I was reminded of this a few years ago when I was looking for something in an aged basement carton. I came across an old, crushed, heart-shaped valentine box. "What is this?," I wondered to myself? I opened the beat up box and it was full of empty brown colored holders for the chocolates it once contained. I was ready to toss it, when I noticed a small tan-colored envelope beneath the brown papers. I pulled out the note inside and recognized the artistic writing of my college boyfriend. "You are a rare bird and I love you immensely," the note said. "Words would wilt if I had to use them to tell you how much." I recalled how deeply that note moved me then, and still. But, while the words lasted, the affection did not. Like so many of our loves and our relationships, it was ephemeral. That painful lesson is one most of us learn at various times in our lives, the often fleeting nature of affection.

These days, I think more of the depth of love that is solid and that lasts through the years. Shared experiences. A quiet look across a room that communicates a moment of happiness or of grief. A person to be with you through the joys and sorrows of it all. Someone to stand by you as you stand by him. In a 1960's magazine article, an author reflects on the beauty of those relationships that have stood the test of time. She wrote, "When I think back, it is not the young love I admire but the long-time affection I find dearer." Me, too. It is the affection I find dearer.

I thought of this recently as I was buried under the covers of my bed with chills in a two week cough-fever-cold-headache-everything else flu. My husband walked into the room quietly to empty the wastebasket that was overflowing with used Kleenex, or to bring me some fresh ice water, or to ask if I needed anything, to which I was too weak to do anything but nod my head. Sometimes, love means emptying the wastebasket, I thought to myself from somewhere in my foggy head. Sometimes it means inconveniencing your own life for the sake of someone you love. And, quite often, it just means being there. And listening.

Love is a precarious thing in its machinations over the years. We move from grade school crushes, to the heartbreaks of love along the way, and then, if we are lucky, to something more solid and substantial that may even last a lifetime.

As love goes, many secrets stay inside. Remembered childhood valentines. Misplaced love letters. And the day someone brings you a glass of ice water and you consider what love really means. We don't always say so, but we know.

For all of the highs and the lows of it, love in its many forms is a lifelong journey. In February, we reflect on the depth and wonder of it all.

For where we would we be without love?

The Bats of Our Minds

It was a small town in Wisconsin in the 1950's. Fond du Lac. I later learned its meaning, "Far end of the lake." It was a good town for a little girl to be growing up in. We lived in a big old gray house with white trim and a huge screened-in front porch, a kind of home you rarely see anymore. It sat in the center of the block in a middle class neighborhood. And this is some of what I remember.

A huge cherry tree in our back yard with cherries plump and sweet, ready for the eating.

Bats that swirled around that cherry tree in the night sky and the day that one got into the kitchen only to be chased out by my parents swinging brooms.

The steel tubs that my mother would fill up with water for us in our backyard during those humid Wisconsin summers, a poor person's excuse for a pool.

The creaky bunk bed, the darkness of the night, and childhood fears of imagined sins.

The joy of recognizing those new precious words on a page, "Jump, Spot, jump!," words that would lead me into a lifetime of loving books.

The school fair where I could use my allowance money to choose a wrapped package for ten cents.

The big roller iron that stood in our kitchen which I later learned was called a mangle, a daunting machine used for ironing sheets back in those days of tedious women's work.

The penny candy at the corner store where it took so long for us to decide what candy to choose that the storekeeper, to save his time, created surprise bags for us.

The outdoor white chipped wicker rockers where we sometimes ate hot fudge sundaes, so cold and so warm on the tongue, so sweet.

The swinging bench on our enclosed porch where my mom would cover us in a golden-colored puffy comforter, a wedding gift of theirs, while we watched the summer thunderstorms that would make us lifelong lovers of weather, tempests, and the shifting seasons.

As life would have it, my family left that house and that town when I was in second grade, to move to a bigger city. Still, I often think back to that home and how rich the memories of our early childhood are, swirling around like the bats of those long-ago days. As adults, we remember little things like the sweetness of lemonade-filled summer days, juicy cherries on our tongue, porch swings, rainy breezes, and cozy rocking chairs. And we remember the angst of growing up as children, so easily amazed, so wondrously sensitive, so easily hurt.

Bats in our minds, tied together by places and times that live on in who we are.

Memories of those childhood days that will never come again.

Varnished Floors and Time

We just re-varnished the wood floors that wind within our home. Actually, my husband did them mostly, as I traveled through my life of working, going to meetings, and being with family. I offer my help, but my hard-working husband usually prefers to focus on projects himself, rarely talking during them. He is an incredible worker, someone who gets a task and gives it his all, never wavering. He says that he likes things he can do, get done with, and see the finished product....in other words, he prefers hands-on work over more nebulous tasks. I often agree with him, remembering a line from a Ciardi poem in which he writes of his longing for the manual labor of his youth, "I miss this the desked days I go," he writes. Even though I understand the sentiment, I tend to return continuously to "desked days," writing, reading, doing volunteer projects on the computer. It is who I am, just as physical work is who my husband is. It is deeply in us, those things that came with our individual packages.

Our young adult children appreciate my husband's work ethic. He helps them move into apartments, he installs air conditioners, he paints rooms, he performs the miscellany of things young people need as they find their way through the maze of moving on. And he is always there for them, solid and hard-working. They will always remember that.

I never know what I'll be remembered for. Mom is just always there, the one who answers the phone, doles out the advice, comforts the wounds, and allows children to say, "Oh, Mom!" to her. We're the centerpiece of the ongoing commotion, the motor, and, I think, the one most often in charge. It's a weighty role.

Sometimes women complain that - after all their years of helping with scouts and dioramas and bake sales and first loves and applications and heartaches and just being there for everything – that later on in life, the children seem to elevate the father to the place of prominence in the family hierarchy, a fate that seems unfair to women given the consistency of their role in those many years the father worked and was gone so much.

I reflect on this, and understand it. Still, I think it not quite accurate. I believe that, as men age into retirement, they finally have the time they often didn't have to give in a new way to their children and family. It is why retired men so often are drawn like magnets to their grandchildren, just as we grandmothers are. Finally, I think they have the time to simply be there. And they find it refreshing, encouraging, enlightening.

Life is never a contest of who gets the most credit. We women will always be "just mom," the one who's always been there, the one who taught them to use the potty, to read, to live with first heartaches, to apply for jobs, and to endure through it all. Children never forget that because it's in their deepest memories. An older father with time who is crazy about his kids and grandkids can be a new experience for adult children, and a grand one. They can now see in their father more than the worries of jobs and money and schedules and pressures that dominated him for many years.

If we have the gift of long years, we fill so many roles, and the roles change as we move on. To appreciate each one, even with the difficulties they pose, is to live a full life. And so we do best to embrace this journey gently, being grateful each second we are in it.

It is truly a grand adventure. We take it for what it is.

After the Storm

In our yard is a broken, once beautiful 23 foot Norwegian Pine that we picked out and had planted seven years ago in the front of our then newly-built home. It grew rapidly over those seven years, got thin and bare for awhile, and then filled out again this year after treatment with muriatic acid. On Sunday, I walked past it and mumbled, "Good job," imagining I guess that this, my favorite tree could hear, or at least feel, my praise. Sunday night a storm came through as I had never seen before in my many years in Wisconsin. The trees in our front yard and in the woods bent and swayed in the incredible wind, some doubled to the ground. When the terrible storm was over, most of the trees had survived the long beating, but our beautiful "good job" pine that lived through near-death bareness, did not. It lays now, split in half, a shadow of its majestic expanse. Tomorrow, we will have to remove what is left of it. How I will miss it.

We plant so many things in our lives, trees not the least among them. Over time, I grow more and more certain that people who plant have a special understanding of what it is to live and to love. Through the seasons as my husband and I perform our ritual walking of the yard together, the litany goes on. "Look, the cone flowers are opening." "The pinks get fuller every year. "I can't believe I'm trying roses." "The clematis against the garage are so beautiful." "The wildflowers are a little seedy this summer." And on and on it goes.

We would not receive any prizes as great gardeners. We squeeze our gardening between jobs, kids, errands, and the assemblage of details that an often too-busy life holds. Our weeds get too high, our grass sometimes goes too long without cutting, and we can't spend what we would like on trees for our yard. And so each tree purchase is a gift, a gift we watch and nurture and treasure. They are, in fact, often referred to as "the one we got for Father's Day," or "the one we bought with our Christmas money," etc. Thus we appreciate each one deeply, our Colorado Blue Spruces, our Elms, our Red Maples, and the little pine that our 21-year-old daughter got and planted when she was in second grade. They are living testaments to our life as a family.

And so the Norwegian Pine will leave a certain emptiness in us. The bare spot in the front yard will remind us of its passing, but it will remind us of something else. I will remember how I said "good job" to it on the last day it stood whole and well, and of how often it made me consider the value of struggling through the tough times.

During the storm, I called each of our children to see if they were all right. Our youngest, still in high school, was at his job and was the easiest to reach. "Of course," he said, "I'm fine. Did you call for that?," his teenage voice queried. I smiled and understood that he would make the same calls to his children in many years to come. I called our youngest daughter in Milwaukee, and she said that the storm wasn't bad there, and that she was going out with friends for pizza. She was understanding of the call, getting older and appreciating the concern – but still hurried to join her friends, oblivious as only the young can be of possible danger out there. Next, I called our oldest son in Milwaukee. He understood our worry, and we talked about the damage here – trees down, wreckage strewn around the yard, and our fallen tree. He affirmed our daughter's statement that it wasn't so bad in Milwaukee. In fact, they sat on their porch and watched the wind. He reminded me of my love of Wisconsin storms, and how we missed them so much in the years we lived briefly in California. Finally, I called our daughter out west and her husband, not that they had a storm, but because they missed this one. They are, like me, storm lovers who watch the mystery and the magic of the wind, the thunder, even the lightning. I told them this one was awesome, but a bit too scary for unqualified admiration.

And, indeed, the storm that hit us so hard on Sunday – some neighbors also have huge trees down – was a storm like none I remember and none I ever want to see again. It scared me as few storms ever have. And when it was over, I knew what we had lost and what we had kept. What we had lost was my favorite tree, and it will never be replaced (even if we replace it) because it came with our new home and because it was watched and loved through difficult years. But I know, too, what we did not lose. We did not lose that which is, and always will be, most important to us. Our children were safe, going on with their various lives, and understanding on some level that we hold them in our hearts enough to call them during a frightening summer storm. It's a message of love, of growth, of watching, of waiting through the hard times, and of holding on for dear life during the raising of all growing things.

If we can get through the storms, we can get through it all. And what gifts we always find there, after the storm.

Just for Laughs

*Author (far left bottom) with siblings and
some of the cousins, early 1950s*

"Tis to Laugh"

Hats, Toasts, and a Hundred Years

There it was this week in black and white, a magazine article listing ways to achieve a cherished goal of mine. It was entitled, "Eleven Health Habits That Will Help You Live to be 100."

Years ago, there was one centenarian in our family, a great aunt on my father's side who lived – mental ability intact – to the age of 100. When my parents took her out for dinner on her 100th birthday, she commented that, as much as she liked hats, she never wore them anymore. "When you wear a hat," she said, "people think that you are old." At 100, she apparently did not think that she was "old" as attested to by the fact that at her birthday party, she suddenly clicked her drinking glass and got up to give a toast.

Well, I would love to live to be 100 if my brain could stay intact. That is, however, a challenge in my family where Alzheimers got to some of my 90 year old aunts before the age of 100 ever arrived. Still, I'm game for trying to reach 100. So I perused the article. That's when I realized the roadblocks.

First of all, they noted that four things are most important – and this was BEFORE they even got to their "Eleven Health Habits." So I knew I was in trouble prior to even reading the list of eleven. They wrote that you can cut your risk of having a stroke by doing four things – being active for 30 minutes a day, eating five daily servings of fruit and vegetables, and avoiding cigarettes and alcohol. Now, the way I count, that is three things but maybe the article was written by someone over one hundred years of age with Alzheimers.

Anyway, telling someone like myself who mostly writes for a living to exercise for 30 minutes a day is somewhat futile. By the time I get done with my morning writing, I am so tired that I take a nap. Then again, maybe the walk to the couch and the deep breathing count as exercise. And, as far as the fruits and vegetables, five servings a day sounds like a stretch – and I even like vegetables. But since I qualify on the not smoking and drinking criteria, I decided to read their eleven points after all.

Number one, "Don't retire." You tell us that now? After years of 401K planning, advertisements of seniors relaxing on the beaches of the world, all that talk of the golden years? Now that the first wave of baby boomers has hit retirement, you do revisionist history? But, according to the research, there is a glimmer of hope for those of us who have already retired. The article notes that retirees who work on small farms cultivating grapes and vegetables seem to escape the health risks of retirement. I just have to find someone with a little grape farm for sale. And wait for summertime.

Number two, "Floss every day." Wow. I can do that. However, since I didn't do it enough when I was younger, the dental hygienist indicates it may be too late to help very much. It seems to be that way with many things as I get older.

Number three, "Move around." They note in the article that walking is still the best exercise of all for the bones and heart. I stare outside the window at this white, snowy, slippery Wisconsin day, and figure I was born in the wrong place. I am never surprised when places like Phoenix, Arizona rank way up on the list of healthiest cities. Biking, tennis, walking. We Wisconsinites instead wait for the end of winter, which only takes about eight months to arrive.

Number four, "Eat a fiber-rich cereal for breakfast." I have nothing to say to this except, "Does Cherry Pepsi count?"

Number five, "Get enough shut eye." The study recommends at least six hours of sleep at night. Well, I get six hours and then I add a one-to-two hour daily nap just for good measure. The researchers say that those who reach the century mark make sleep a top priority. Since napping is my greatest talent, I have no problem here.

Number six, "Consume whole foods, not supplements." This is a running debate in my household. My husband takes daily doses of mega vitamins and I rarely touch a vitamin pill. I think he's overworking his kidneys and liver and other organs, and he thinks I'm depriving mine of needed nutrients. If this study means anything, this might just be one argument I win.

Number seven – the biggest stumbling block of all for me – "Be less neurotic." Who? Me? I have a husband, four children, four grandchildren, a dog, a house, a car, a truck, a radio program, two columns a month, a rental unit, an overabundance of volunteer commitments, and tea party relatives. Besides that, I am descended from a long line of worriers on my mother's side of the family, and many of those ancestors were single with no children. (What did they have to worry about, I wonder in amazement.) My sister said to me recently mid-sentence, "depending upon what my current worry is." I laughed. It's in our genetic makeup. We were just born this way.

Number eight – "Live like a Seventh Day Adventist." Huh? It turns out that Seventh Day Adventists live an average of a decade longer than the rest of us. And they do it by adhering to this very list – a plant-based diet, no smoking, limited alcohol, limited sweets, regular exercise. So, as a writer, I think they could have left this one off the list and just written "see above and below." Why give the Seventh Day Adventists credit for a list the researchers have allegedly created after much study and review? Besides, if the writer left this off, then the list would be entitled "Ten Health Habits for Living to be 100," not "Eleven Health Habits." Wouldn't that make more sense?

Number nine, "Be a creature of habit." The researchers say that routine is the best thing as we age, same diet, same bedtime, same activities. Hmmm. How do they know that these centenarians might not have lived even longer if they had spiced it up a little? A few adventures, a few nights out, a little less sleep might have done a world of good for them. It could be worth a try.

Number ten, "Stay connected." I quit reading this one because the author called the baby boom generation "elderly" and began writing about "premature death" and "memory loss." We never did take criticism well.

Number eleven, "Be conscientious." You know, take care of your responsibilities, be at your appointments on time, take your pills, blah, blah, blah. After long years, baby boomers (not "the elderly") have pretty much done all of that anyway. We're good.

Despite this lengthy list, the article noted, somewhat ironically I thought, "Of course, getting to age 100 is enormously more likely if your parents did." Well, duh. It said those who had at least one long-lived relative were twenty times as likely as the average person to be centenarians. I could have guessed that. In fact, we could probably just skip the list of four (or three) and the list of eleven and just trust our gene pool, and it might all come out the same. Who knows?

So, since I do have one precedent for a long life, I might try for that century mark after all. Just as long as I don't have to give up Cherry Pepsi to get there.

And on my 100th birthday, I think I'll wear a hat, give a toast, and try not to spill my soda.

Time for a Nap

Sometime before his death, commentator Andy Rooney was asked in an interview how long it took him to write a column. He said, in his avuncular way, something like, "The good ones take an hour. The bad ones take weeks." When I heard that, I laughed out loud, thinking how true that is. Of course, with all of the editing and re-editing, no good column is written in one hour. Still, there is truth to the fact that the "good ones" seem to flow onto the paper while the "bad ones" are almost painful to write, and end up being trashed after weeks in the making.

I mentioned to a friend that I didn't know what to write my next column about, and she said, "Write one on naps. Naps are terribly underrated." Needing a nap myself at the time after a Thanksgiving week in which twelve people came in and out of the house for seven days, with four of them being ages 11, 8, 5, and 3, it sounded like a compelling topic. I thought about it and took a nap.

Robert Fulghum wrote an essay about what he should put on his business card. Should he put "minister" or "writer" or "father" or "philosopher," he pondered? He wrote that maybe he actually should put "napper" on the card because he considered that napping was one of the things he did best. He ended up just putting the word "Fulghum" on it rather than try to summarize in a word who he was. Still, I never forgot his napper comment, probably because napping is one of the things I do best also.

For all of the years when we had four very young children, I was never able to get enough sleep. I remember being pregnant with the next one and thinking that I'd go out on the street and pay someone to watch the kids while I napped. Once I even called my sister from out of town and she came over so I could sleep. I wish I had just made that up, but it's actually true.

There were days during pregnancy when I remember lining the kids up in front of the television and begging them to watch TV while I went into a semi-sleep in an easy chair in the room. Anyone who has been pregnant knows that you are never as tired as you are when you're expecting. Once a day I could have laid down anywhere, even on a cactus bed, and gone to sleep upon command. Of course, watching the kids always ended up trumping the naps in those busy days, so I was continuously sleep deprived. I don't think, to this day, that I've ever really caught up from that sleep deprivation.

"Ah sleep! It is a gentle thing/Beloved from pole to pole!/To Mary Queen the praise be given!/She sent the gentle sleep from heaven,/That slid into my soul," Coleridge wrote in *Rime of the Ancient Mariner*. And he was, presumably, never even pregnant!

Once the kids were all in school and I only worked part time, I sometimes could sneak in a short nap and I remember still thinking how unbelievably refreshing that was. I remember wishing that I could have sent those naps back in time to that poor, pregnant woman I had been who never got enough sleep. Still, my napping days were brief as I began fulltime work.

Now that I am retired, I finally get to nap, and I relish every single second of those naps. I think we sleep better and deeper in one hour on the couch in the afternoon than we do all night long in our beds. There's something about an afternoon nap.

My best naps happen at 3:30 in the afternoon when Jeopardy is on. I lie on the couch, fully intending to watch the program, and I often do get half way through it before I doze. My daughter asked once, "Why aren't you better at Jeopardy since you watch it all the time?" I didn't tell her that I actually don't see much of the program.

Busy executives have talked about "power naps," and I've always believed there is something to that. I notice that as I get older, I often wake up at 4 am and, instead of forcing myself back to sleep, I read a book or go to the computer or do some work. I assume that my body is just done sleeping for the time being, and that I have the luxury of being able to nap later. I've wondered if, as we age, our body senses that being awake for more time in the years we have left might be a good idea. And many people do their best work in the early hours of dawn.

The inventor Thomas Edison spoke of how he never really slept in one stretch at night, but that he instead would work on a project until he got tired and then he'd lay down to sleep. When he woke up after a short time quite refreshed, he would go back to his work. So maybe our pattern of sleeping one long stretch is really not the best model for creativity.

While I like the Edison model for sleep, I think employees might have trouble with implementing it on the job site. I can almost hear an employee explaining how Edison had inspired him, and I can hear the response of the boss. "You, John, are no Thomas Edison. Get back to work!"

I read once of an employee who would retreat to a closet at work in the afternoons for a power sleep. He was caught at his cat napping, and he was fired that very day. At the time, I was horrified at the laziness of taking work time to sleep in a closet, but now I think there may be some sense in it. Maybe he was an Edison in the making.

Well, this column wrote up pretty quickly which, according to Andy Rooney, could mean that it's good. Then again, it might just mean that I'm so sleep deprived that I could go on writing about sleep forever. And I could, except that I'm getting tired. I think it's time for my afternoon nap.

I hope you can get one, too.

Walking to O'Hare....

Okay, here's a funny story. Except that it really happened, which makes it a not-so-funny-story. And it really happened to me, which makes it an especially not-so-funny-story. And it happened in an airplane, which makes it a really, really scary story.

Awhile back, my husband and I boarded a plane to return home to Wisconsin from a warmer clime. I will omit the name of the carrier, except to report that it was a major airline, not Two-Men-and-a-Plane or On-a-Wing-and-a-Prayer Flights or Fly-By-Night Airlines. The scheduled departure time was 8:50 a.m. and yet, twenty minutes later we were still sitting in the grounded airplane, waiting for takeoff. And, as any of us fear-phobic flying people will tell you, any delay in takeoff or landing is enough to make us ponder end-of-life questions.

At 9:15 a.m., the pilot came over the intercom with a message. Now, this is never good news. It is particularly never good news to those of us who cannot bring ourselves to believe that a huge metal container filled with over a hundred people and their baggage was ever meant to leave the ground much less fly through the air. Forget the statistics on the safety of flying versus driving. Forget that Leonardo da Vinci somehow knew all those years ago that flying craft would be a reality someday. Forget that I can't remember the last time a commercial airliner crashed. It is just not natural to fly.

My husband, who has flown all over the world points out calmly that we spend a lot more for plane fare because I require direct flights without multiple connections. And he's right. If I have to fly, it's a get-on-this-thing-and-don't-think-about-it kind of experience.

So, I was as prepared as I could be for yet another trek when the pilot, who clearly had never been provided the mandatory we-all-sound-the-same communication course, spoke to us. "Well, you're probably wondering why we haven't taken off yet. Turns out that one of our baggage handlers looked up and noticed a piece of metal protruding from one of our wings, and so we're having maintenance inspect the wing to determine if the plane can make another leg. I'll report back to you as soon as we know something."

Panic and what-in-the-heck-is-going-on thoughts went whirling through my head. I looked around to view everyone else's reaction and was surprised that they just went on with their reading or eating or resting. A guy across the aisle from me noticed my anxiety and reacted. "Well," he said, "that was more information than we needed." I got up the courage to ask him, "How can we fly if metal is protruding from the wing?" "Oh," he responded, "don't worry. I work with planes and this isn't all that unusual. It happens."

It happens. Okay, I thought as I tried to settle into a "we won't really crash" state of mind. Since our seats were right behind the wing, though, it was less possible to relax as we watched a lift carry some ordinary looking guys up to inspect the damage. Another twenty minutes later, the captain's voice came over the loudspeaker again.

"Well," he said in his folksy way, "Great news to report. The wing has been inspected and we will be able to take off following repairs. There is some damage, but they will be running across the street to get some epoxy and some speed tape and our wing will be repaired in a jiffy." I swear I am not making this up – he said "running across the street." To where, I wondered? Home Depot? Wal-Mart? Menards?

I looked at the man-who-works-with-airplanes on my left and asked questions I was afraid I knew the answer to. "Why epoxy? What's speed tape? Where are they running across the street to?"

"Well," he responded, "epoxy is like super glue and speed tape is like duct tape only" – the next to appease me – "much, much stronger. Believe me, this is not all that unusual."

Perhaps not, but his words were of small comfort to me as my mind raced. What about the duct tape that falls off of our Christmas cartons each year, even without flying hundreds of miles through the air? What if Home Depot has a shortage of super glue? What if they use Elmer's by mistake? What if they only have duct tape and not speed tape? Isn't there another plane we could take? Couldn't I just walk to O'Hare?

My mind raced through every airplane crash I had seen depicted in movies. I phoned our adult children, getting all of their answering machines. "Hi," I said cheerily, "we've been a little delayed but we'll be on our way home soon. I just called to say I love you."

I looked around again and saw that people were still reading their books, dozing, or calling about the delay. To my amazement, no one was deplaning. Twenty minutes later, just as I was about to deplane, the pilot cheerily reported that we were going to take off momentarily. "Off we go," he chirped.

And, yes, we did take off with the shiny silver speed tape very visible to me from my close up seat behind the wing. Needless to say, we made it safely to O'Hare airport. And I am a wiser person for the experience. I now know that they tape plane wings together in an emergency, a fact I never would have imagined even in my most frightened, I-hate-to-fly states of mind, a fact I really didn't need to know. I now know that not all pilots have gone through the "We're experiencing a few difficulties but should be taking off soon" communication course. And I now know that, if we were meant to fly, we would have been given wings.

Next time, maybe walking to O'Hare wouldn't be such a bad idea.

Growing Older

Author's Grandma Lavinia, circa 1900, born 1883

"I am not afraid of storms for I am learning to sail my ship."
— Louisa May Alcott

Dressing the Part

"You always wear black," an acquaintance said to me many years ago.

Surprisingly, that was the first time I had ever thought about it, not being much interested in clothing. "I guess that's true, isn't it?," I mumbled almost to myself.

She went on to opine, as if she had given this some prior thought, "I think it's probably because so many of your teachers wore black in elementary school."

I didn't agree, but I made no response. Being one who lives in a world of my own invented theories, I couldn't blame her for coming up with her own. And it is true that, especially when I have a meeting or a presentation or a party to attend, I do tend to come to the event dressed in one of the many black dresses I have collected through the machinations of my life.

I have noticed through the years that I am not the only one who gravitates toward black clothing. Newscaster Rachel Maddow, whom I greatly admire, is almost always in black. And I learned from a historical re-enactor that Susan B. Anthony was seen just about exclusively in black, except when she diverged with her red cape or red jackets. And, of course, there was Johnny Cash, the "man in black." Since there is an entire chain of clothing stores called "Black and White," we must be a dedicated but considerable tribe.

It is an interesting phenomenon, this tendency toward black. Is it a trend to the dramatic that makes us choose black? Is it our shyness, and a wish not to stand out? Or is it just simpler to have black clothing that you can wear with colored scarves or ties? I don't know, but I like the first reason the best for Susan B. Anthony was certainly someone dramatic who fought uphill battles for challenging causes. We all hope that, at various times in our lives, we have done the same. She is good company to be among.

I rarely shop for clothes these days. In retirement, I'm mostly in jeans and tops, black, of course. And I still have a closet full of "good clothes" from my days of work in a professional environment. Now, on those rare occasions like today when I do go shopping, I lecture myself silently before I leave home just as I did on this day. "You will not buy a black dress. You will think color. Maybe red. Maybe green. Maybe blue. You will not buy black." The scolding rarely works.

And so today as I stood in the store, my eyes gravitated to something I really liked. "What a cute dress," I thought to myself as I walked toward the rack. Then I realized what it was. A black dress. Another black dress. But it was *so cute.*

Growing older, they say, is not for the faint of heart. I understand the wisdom of that more and more as the years go by. There is so much that is difficult about it. Aching joints you never knew you had. A mind that forgets things it shouldn't. And eyes that don't see as clearly as they once did. (Although some of that is a blessing, the poignant irony of your vision weakening just as the wrinkles begin to line your face.)

Yet for all of the negatives of growing old - and there are many - there are gifts as well. One of the best, I think, it that we know ourselves better. We look back and we see things more clearly. We see our mistakes and our successes, and we realize how hard we have been trying all along. We're more comfortable with who we are and where we've been. And we understand that, while we did not accomplish all that we wanted to, we didn't do too badly, either. It's been a good journey.

And so that ultimate gift of aging, that gift of finally knowing who we are, comes in handy as time passes. We comprehend the beauty of a strong friendship. We marvel in the younger generation moving forward with hope and promise and the future in their faces.

And we know, with a gentle self-acceptance, that we are who we are, idiosyncrasies and all.

And so today, I glanced at the clothing rack once again and went back to get that black dress after all.

It suits me just fine.

Mistakes and Genetics

I made a big mistake this week. I am a hard worker and I pride myself on thoroughness and diligence. Still, for whatever reason, I missed something important.

Mistakes are frightening things when you're the one making them. You wonder if you're getting old. You wonder if your mind isn't as sharp as it once was. You think that maybe you had let yourself become distracted. And, especially when your mistake affects others, you worry for those who paid a price, however small, for your error.

I have a reason for worrying about mistakes. My genetic pattern most closely resembles that of my mom's family and I am like they were in looks and mannerisms. They were a lively family of people who laughed a lot and talked about ideas, politics, history. Except for war, illness and accidents with three of my mother's nine siblings, the others lived long lives, especially the women, most of whom survived to around 90 years of age. I remember their faces and their alacrity and the brightness of their eyes. They were of good stock.

And then, in their final years, something happened to my maternal grandmother and some of my aunts. They became sad and confused. They forgot the names of friends and sometimes even family. They couldn't remember the days of the week, who was President, what season it was. They could no longer take care of themselves, they did frightening things like handing out their valuables to strangers in store parking lots. They spent their last years in nursing homes among people they didn't know but thought they did. It is the fate we most fear, this fate of theirs, and it is rampant today. One in 8 of Americans over the age of 65 and half of those over 85 have the disease. It is the 6th leading cause of death in the US and the 5th leading cause for those over 65. And it has a name – Alzheimers Disease.

My mother and her siblings talked with enormous affection about their mother, my grandmother, a woman who, when she had ten young children, saw her hard-working husband die suddenly before her eyes. She went on to raise the children alone, getting them to productive adulthood. My grandmother was a strong women and she found ways to support and educate her children. (My mother remembers lard sandwiches during the depression.) When a son died in his teens of spinal meningitis, she carried on for the others. When another son, a gifted pianist, a humorist, and the beloved baby of the family, died at 20 years of age in World War II, she once again carried on for the others.

Yes, my grandmother was an amazing woman, and her children spoke of her strength and courage. But my memories of her are different. I was young when she died, but I remember her as someone who couldn't focus, someone who looked lost in a room, someone whose eyes stared blankly into mine. She was my grandma and I tried to connect, but something was missing. In my memory she sits blankly, quietly, and only the stories of her children let me know who she was.

I have a snapshot of my grandmother taken a few years before she died and it confirms my memory of her. She is standing as if confused holding a tilting plate in the middle of a kitchen filled with her family members. Her eyes capture a look of fear, confusion, and vagueness. Even a casual viewer of that photo would guess that she wasn't certain where she was.

I asked my mother once about my image of her mother and she said she never saw that. Perhaps because my grandmother's children had gone through so many years with her, they held inside of themselves a lifelong picture of the strong woman she was, blinding them mercifully to the confused person she became. Maybe it is good that people love us early on because that love carries them through the difficult times that we all arrive at one way or another.

Hers is the fate, though, that I and others fear is in our genes. We've seen it and it terrifies us, makes our blood go cold. We don't want our children struggling with us at a stage when they need to introduce us to people we've known for years. We don't want them burdened, nor do we want to be burdened with final years like that. It is too painful.

Periodically, we hear that researchers have identified a gene, or come up with a new drug, or have hope for a cure for the dreaded disease of Alzheimers. In the meantime, little mistakes pose an enormous threat to our psyches, especially for those of us with dementia in our backgrounds. When we forget names or phone numbers, put things in the wrong drawer, or wake up taking a moment to adjust, we freeze briefly in fear and ask ourselves questions we don't have answers for. Would we have done this when we were 30? Is it just a mistake from an overly busy life? And, most importantly, is there anything we can do? And we stand mute without answers, as alone in a room of people as my grandma was in her own kitchen those many years ago.

I know one thing. I have seen the fate of my grandmother and my aunts, and it isn't a fate I choose. I will watch, be diligent, and hope that I have choices before my mind takes the possibility of choice away. In the meantime, I plan to continue as they did, living a full life, appreciating every moment, laughing, and knowing that this journey is so wondrous and so worthwhile that continuing it while we can is the only reasonable path to take.

Someday, they will find a cure for this horrible disease. Maybe even in time for us.

Turning the Pages

I will always miss it. The crinkle of the plastic library book covers. The turning of the paper pages of a book. Underlining my favorite parts. Holding the book against me as I reflect or rest for a moment. I am, in fact, often found asleep with a book resting across me. It's part of the reading experience for me, the book itself.

E-books are selling as never before. Some schools have gone entirely without textbooks in favor of electronic books. It is the future, I understand, and not to embrace the future is to slowly enclose yourself in darkness and to become hopelessly buried in what was. Those who rail against the future cannot help but lose.

I recently purchased an e-book for myself, and I like it a great deal. I am far too much of a realist not to know that life moves on, "nor tarries with yesterday." Still, I think it's the tactile experience I will miss the most as I venture, along with the rest, into a world with fewer and fewer books and more and more turning of icon pages on electronic screens. Not that I think books will ever be completely gone. But we are increasingly tuning into an on-screen reading world.

The bookstore is a favorite haunt of mine. Bookstores are so magic now, the soft music, the comfortable couches, the coffees, the slow pace that allows you to sit and read and browse with no one wondering why you are hanging around for so long. I knew someone who years ago fell in love in a bookstore, glancing up from the world of reading into the eyes of a fellow reader. It never surprised me. What better place to fall in love than there, buried in all of that quiet and peace? But I wonder. Will there be bookstores in the new age of electronic books? Or will it be one of the casualties that come with change?

I have friends who, like me, have also gotten electronic books, and they like them far more than they thought they would. They are my age (kindly we say) in the autumn of our lives. It is a time of life we truly like, if we could just stay here. Fewer ups and downs, and more quiet acceptance of who we are, where we've been, what we've built, what we love. We're not afraid of the future because we've seen so much of change. The coming of computers into our homes. ("What will we do with computers in our homes?," we once naively wondered.) The coming of microwaves. ("Will we get cancer from those waves bumping about?") The coming of emails allowing us to send digital photos across the country. ("How is that possible?," we pondered.) People my age have seen more innovations and changes develop in our life-times than any other generation. (When my late mother was born, women couldn't even vote!) We can scarcely imagine what the future will hold. We've seen so much that now, anything seems possible.

I remember a reporter telling me a funny story about newsrooms. He said that when computers entered the newsroom, many reporters and edi-tors clung furiously to their old typewriters, plucking away for months or years before giving in to this "new computer thing." He said that the same was true of newspaper photographers when digital cameras came to be. Eventually these reporters, editors, and photographers came to see the beauty of the new tools at their disposal. And so it is as the future moves in. We see its potential.

I am getting older, but I am not among those who are pessimistic about the future. I think of all the advantages of the world today. We can fly across the country to see family and friends in journeys that would have taken our ancestors months to complete. Television, while often banal, also gives us an enormous wealth of news and information. Young people benefit tremen-dously in their education from the wonders of the internet. The world is richer now than it ever was, and the future will be richer still. And the great mystery of being a child will always be the great mystery of being a child.

Still, there's this book thing. I love books the way they've always been, almost an art form in themselves as the 19th century publisher and writer Elbert Green Hubbard taught us years ago. And so my basement stash of books will stay as it is, with old books from college, novels I've read over the years, and the classics with their ageless truths. I'll keep them as a reminder of magic as we progress to the new age of electronic reading.

Life moves on, and we know it. And so we will leave that future to our kids, our grandkids, our descendants – just as our ancestors let go to leave it to us. I'll leave it with some sorrow, though, as it's been quite a journey. And I hate to miss what is to come, the endless change of seasons, the new waves of innovations yet to be invented, and the beautiful young people still to come, still to create, still to live out their dreams. "Oh, brave new world that has such people in it."

I imagine that new generations will love their electronic books just as we love turning the paper pages of our worn books. Life is really just what it always has been, turning the pages from one book to the next, from one generation to another. And it is, with all of its changes, an incredible story, this book of life that we read.

I wouldn't trade that for anything.

In the Sea of Christmas

I look around at the remaining clutter in the room late on Christmas night, the family having gone to bed, myself sitting alone by the holiday lights, sipping warm cocoa, finally relaxing after the noise of Christmas day.

I stare at the room. Some torn red and silver wrapping paper is in the corner, rubbish now that wasn't picked up earlier by those stuffing crinkled paper into black plastic garbage bags. A few cups with dried up punch around the rims sit neglected. ("Don't worry, I'll get the rest of it," I had told them. "Go to bed.") New toys for the grandkids lie scattered under the tree, ready for tomorrow's packing to be transported with love back to their homes where they will be played with and, eventually, discarded.

It was a happy day this Christmas, mostly smiles and laughter and joy that we could be together, mostly an understanding that the being together was the best part of this, or of any, day. And I am satisfied and stilled by the clear, steady holiday lights.

Within the next few days, we will take down for another year the tree, the holly, the mistletoe, the wreaths, the Santas, the trappings. It is strange to look at the assortment of things around me and to remember how much of life is about filling rooms up and eventually emptying them, about beginning journeys and then ending them, about accumulating and finally letting go. It is a parody of a long life. It is, in fact, the lesson of a long life.

I have a friend who has lived a busy, mission packed, fulfilling existence. Yet, after all these years of doing so much, she is mulling it over, thinking of leaving her job for retirement, wondering what will be left when she faces herself and quieter times ahead.

I don't know what to tell her. No matter how many people we have in our lives, we all ultimately journey alone, and we never know what lies before us on any path we take. But we do know this. We seem to find something when we slowly empty the rooms, let go of the clamor, clear away the debris. I remember a haunting line from an e.e. cummings poem, "but whatever we've lost, like a you or a me, it is always ourselves that we find by the sea."

What I find this peaceful Christmas night is just that, I realize. Sitting in the stillness, I know the truth of the hubbub of the holidays and of the quieter winter days to come. It is ourselves that we find as we journey forward, letting go of much, and holding on to even more.

And here, alone by my own sea, I understand.

It is enough.

With All of Your Heart

We finally get to do it. All of us parents and teachers and mentors who have kept our words to ourselves as much as we could stand to during the adolescent years of our children, trying hard not to tell them what to do all of the time, can finally speak up. Our seniors are graduating now, and we can at last give them advice. Because graduates understand, as we do, that this really is a turning point, one of those remarkable times in life when we can really see that life is taking a sharp bend in the road. Like marriage, or a new career, or starting a family, graduation is a time to realize that nothing will be quite the same ever again. It is a time for reflection. And so we adults can say, "Now daughter, this is what life has taught me." "Now, son, this is what I have learned."

There is a great little book from years ago that is called, "Live, Learn, and Pass It On." The author simply asked people of all ages to complete the phrase, "I have learned that..." Some responses are profound like that of a middle-aged person who wrote, "I have learned that you can never have too many kind people in your life." And other responses are humorous like that of a six-year-old who wrote, "I have learned that you cannot hide your broccoli in a glass of milk." Wisdom comes to us in many forms. Back when I taught creative writing, I sometimes used the phrase "I have learned that..." as a writing warmup for students and it produced surprisingly wise and funny results. For those who mentor or teach youth or even adults, it is something you may want to try.

Another way to do much the same thing is by writing your own list of recommendations for life and asking your young people to write theirs. Not rigid rules, but recommendations. In doing so, you may discover some of your own core beliefs and concepts. You might even want to turn your recommendations into a card for your special graduate. Being the thinkers that young people are, they won't take all of your advice, and they shouldn't. We are all our own people, and our uniqueness is part of the wonder of it all. Still, some of your wisdom will stick, and these young people may just quote you in years to come.

So, here I go, like so many adults this time of year, saying simply to young people....here are my recommendations. Use what feels right to you on your journey, and discard the rest.

* Hold inside your heart the things you have always loved. They are what you are about.

* Never stop planting things that grow, whether they be flowers, ideas or possibilities.

* Listen deeply to the very young and the very old. They hold the secrets of forever in their stories.

* Love something so much that it hurts.

* Learn something new every single day. And tell someone about it.

* Be kind to yourself. You know how hard you are trying. And be kind to others. Chances are that they're doing the same.

* At least once a year, watch the sun rise and the sun set. Beginnings and endings and continuity tell the truest story.

* Don't take yourself too seriously. But don't take yourself too lightly. You may not realize it, but you are far more important to others than you will ever know.

* Laugh often. People who laugh keep warmth and youth in their spirit.

* Be principled. Live what you believe.

* Step over the ant. In your next life, she may be your boss.

* Listen to your own voice as much as the voice of experts. Your heart knows what you should do.

* Don't let your own hurt turn into bitterness. Know that hurt, if well used, can help you grow.

* Even if you aren't religious, be spiritual. Spirit is deeper than religion.

* Find a place each day where you can sit perfectly still, alone. Close your eyes. Listen to the quiet.

* Rejoice. Yesterday's mistakes are yesterday's mistakes. Forgive yourself and begin again.

* Don't put limits on your own possibilities. You can do anything. You can be anything. So draw, learn, dance, paint, sing, grow. You are a miracle. Discover it every day.

* Be grateful. Whatever we have or do not have in this life, simply to be alive every day of this very short, very sweet existence is truly a miracle. We are abundantly blessed.

We journey on our own, but the wise counsel of those who have preceded us is not to be taken lightly. So, sail off, graduates, be brave, and move forward with hope. And remember the sage advice of another fellow traveler, Confucius, who said, "Wherever you go, go with all of your heart."

With all of your heart.

The Destination

My baby's getting married in June. Of course, he is no baby, twenty-nine in fact, a lovely man, smart and kind and talented, marrying a lovely girl. But, as moms everywhere understand, they are always our babies, these children of ours.

The wedding is happy news, news that we believe will last a lifetime. They laugh together, a lot. It's what seems best to me about the two of them. They make each other laugh. And there are many other signs of their unity. They hold on to each other a lot also, and they both love the music which he writes and plays on piano, guitar, and synthesizer. And she plays piano as well. When they are at our home, the music is profound. Music and laughter are in their souls. It is a good beginning.

As we get older, we realize how young we were when we married, beginning on a journey of so many twists and turns and ups and downs that we cannot even imagine it at its start. There is so much ahead of us, and yet we jump into marriage with a sheer leap of faith in the substance of our love. We will make it, we're sure, and we don't need to know all of the details ahead. It is an adventure, after all, this life we live.

A young couple we knew were married last year, and it was a destination wedding. In the fall before the wedding, the soon-to-be bride and groom had traveled to a national monument in the mountains near Tucson, Arizona exploring the area as a possible future wedding site. The rocky crags were breathtaking, the blue sky crystalline, the desert climate warm, embracing. And so they chose to be married outdoors the following spring on this southwestern mountain employing the various shades of turquoise, the spiritual Indian words, the rocky terrain, and the light feathers of birds of the area. It was a carefully considered decision to be married at that monument, in that place, and in their own time. They knew what they wanted.

Yet, the wedding did not come off without its hitches. First of all, the weather refused to cooperate and, in a week of Tucson sunny 70's, it plunged into a record low temperature for the wedding day with nippy winds and a forecast of rain. Secondly, on the day before their wedding the federal government threatened to shut down at midnight. The bride was in tears when she received a call informing her that, if the government closed, the wedding site would not be available. Thirdly, a major airline experienced a hole in the top of one of its planes while in flight, causing a fleet of planes to be grounded delaying flights in Arizona. Some wedding guests were worried about arriving at all. And, almost to add insult to injury, the nearby municipality closed for repairs the only highway leading to the ranch from 9 pm the night before the wedding to 9 am the following morning, giving any late-arriving guests a 67-mile detour. It certainly seemed to the young couple like the fates were conspiring against them for the most important day of their lives. The bride wept real tears.

But, as most stories go, things worked themselves out. Most importantly, the government did not shut down. The guests arrived on their flights with few if any delays. All guests arrived in time to avoid the highway closure. And the weather, while very cool and windy, did not produce the predicted rainfall. And so we guests were able to take the 20 minute hike up the mountain to view the ceremony and to be witnesses to this union of a bride and groom on this special day, at this special place, and in their own time.

It was a tribute to the bride how bravely she stood on that windy, cold mountaintop in her strapless, short dress, feathers in her hair and cowboy boots on her feet, saying her vows smoothly with the passion and determination of the true heroine she was. And it was a tribute to the groom who looked at her with such love and admiration in his eyes, keeping her steady, his words promising a lifetime of commitment and togetherness. We were honored to be listeners.

The message of the day was not lost on the older ones among us who had climbed our own mountains together on our own cold and rocky paths. Plans often fall through, trails are often rough, and the sun does not always shine. But journeys are the whole of it, and that's what marriage and life teaches us. It felt like a parody of a long life, climbing up those mountains to look down on the struggles endured and the wholeness of it all. It is a message of what happens along this uneven journey in which we so often face the surprise of the things that happen, as they say, "while we are making other plans."

Like the bride and the groom on that cool Arizona day, we do best when we embrace the journey for what it is. "For better or for worse," as those vows proclaim. All of the guests on the mountaintop that Arizona day knew that the couple had taken their first and most important steps together. And now they, like my son and his wife, and like partners everywhere, just need to step carefully through the rocks of their days, enjoying the sunny days and the cloudy ones, and embracing the journey for all that it is worth.

That is a destination worth achieving.

Holes in the Sky

It can happen. It does, in fact, happen to people every day.

A wife kisses her husband goodbye as he goes off to run in the Boston Marathon. Later she learns that there has been another tragic, senseless bombing. The wife will never kiss her husband again or be with him.

Parents put their children on a bus to visit a college and are told later in the day that there was an accident. Some of those parents will never see their children again.

A woman in a hurry to get to an event is hit by a driver who goes through a stop light. She is taken by ambulance to the Intensive Care Unit. She dies a day later, kept alive mechanically so that her family can arrive to say their goodbyes. The family of the beloved woman is in shock.

As we get older, we reflect on how we are spending our time. How many years do we have left? Thirty? Twenty? Ten? A week? It becomes more important to us to consider how we spend the moments of our lives that we have left. Even without a tragic ending, we have limited time here. Whether we are twenty or sixty, our days are measured. Yet it is often only as we reach our later years that we start thinking about how we are using the moments we have. We know it's important.

Arianna Huffington wrote a book recently entitled *Thrive*. As I was perusing it, I realized how often recently I have been thinking about the same concept she has been considering. We came to it by different life events, both life-changing. For Huffington, it was finding herself face down on the floor, bleeding on her head from hitting her desk on the way down. After getting help, she was diagnosed with exhaustion and stress. Out of that life event, she began thinking about her life, her success, and how she had been spending her time.

Success, she postulates, in our culture equates primarily with material goods and power. It is, she summarizes, like trying to live on a two-legged stool. You can balance for awhile, but you will always eventually fall off. And money and power evaporate in meaning when we die. Legacy does not.

When I was in college, I loved the following quote. "The fallacy of Western civilization lies in its belief that happiness comes about through the accumulation of material goods and leisure time when, in fact, happiness only comes about through the pursuit of meaningful goals."

Meaningful goals. That's what we really seek as we get older. And now we have a better definition of the word meaningful.

Meaningful is spending a day outside, all alone, watching clouds, and reading a book, and breathing deeply and quietly.

Meaningful is holding in your hands a piece of clay and molding into a work of your own creation.

Meaningful is a day with dear friends who sometimes know you better than your know yourself.

Meaningful is being with the children and grandchildren who fill your heart.

Meaningful is about connections, to other people, to our earth, and especially to ourselves. Those are sacred places, and those are the places out of which legacy comes.

I have been on many committees over the years, and I hope that my presence made those groups a little more impactful. But now, I am pulling away and seeking direction from my inner light. I want to live something that lasts. Georgia O'Keefe wrote of that, "I want art that makes holes in the sky."

No one can tell anyone else where their meaning lies, but we all know it when we find it. We know when we are in meaningful places and when we are not. A luxury of getting older is that we can choose to a greater extent than ever before. We've been where we've been, we've lived what we've lived, and we – finally – are who we are.

Finding our most authentic path is now our choice.

And we know it.

Release

Last week, my mother-in-law died. In a death from cancer that dragged on for what seemed like an eternity to her, she finally, mercifully, was able to let go. Those of us who loved her wished, for her sake, that it could have been sooner.

Hers was not the first death from cancer I have witnessed in recent years. Two years ago, my father-in-law passed away of cancer, and six months later, my own father. We watched them suffer and felt the helplessness of being there with little we could do, no way to help.

I remember my father, sweet and dear to the end, asking us with some embarrassment in the final months of his life to help him get his socks on. It hurt him to bend over. In our misguided love, we had continued to try to talk him into getting dressed and moving around. It was our useless hope that somehow he could beat the odds, that, if he tried hard enough, he'd survive the cancer monster devouring him. It was a futile wish, of course, and ultimately we accepted that truth. In the end, he was hospitalized and an IV drip made his death somewhat more bearable, somewhat less agonized. But his final days hurt him terribly, and we knew it. And we watched.

I remember putting our dog to sleep. It was something I had never believed in doing. But Rags was old, had not eaten in two weeks and seemed to have, in the last few days, stopped drinking water, too. On the morning I took him to the veterinarian, he was not able to push himself up on his legs. It was too much, even for one wanting to keep him alive. I picked up my little friend and carried him off to the vet who delivered him to a merciful death. Held in my arms, he was given a shot. What happened next I will never forget. Without a whimper, without a cry, in what was only seconds, his limp head sank down on my arm and it was over. I could not forget, will never forget the seeming peacefulness of that death.

I listen with pause to the passionate debate over euthanasia, Oregon's Death with Dignity Law, and the actions of the late Dr. Kevorkian, and I understand the arguments of the critics. Why should mere humans decide the ultimate question of life and death? Why should we determine when the final goodbye takes place and the final breath is taken? Who are we to decide things so momentous? And those arguments are logical and compelling.

But I have watched death now and its shameless realities. And I know, too, that truth is found in tricky places, hiding always between the easy answers, buried in those shadowed areas between the black and the white. And so I have no answers. All I really know is that I hope, when the end is near for me, that I get the time my father had to tell us that he loved us and to repeat, over and over, what a lucky person he had been. But I hope, too, that beyond those meaningful moments, that there may be someone to deliver me, as mercifully as I delivered my little friend, beyond the longer days of meaningless pain and suffering.

It just may just be the best and most important gift we can give to another human being, a final gift to one whom we have loved. A final, peaceful farewell.

Taking Care Of Ourselves

Author with Neighborhood Friend, circa 1950

"Be kind to yourself.
The world is full of critics. Help yourself become.
You know how hard you are trying."
Author's Journal Entry

The Power of Quiet

I was in the bookstore this week, and a book by Susan Cain captured my attention immediately with its title alone. *Quiet*. I picked it up and perused it, and the intrigue deepened. It was subtitled, "The Power of Introverts in a World That Can't Stop Talking."

It reminded me of a funny quote I had heard the week before. "If other people are going to talk, conversation becomes almost impossible!" How often have we been with – or have ourselves been – a person who doesn't stop talking. Even introverts, in particular situations, can be among those who talk too much. Being basically an introvert myself, I know that very well.

Everyone loves extroverts. They entertain us, make us laugh, and can lead a room with their presence and passion. Yet I have always been drawn to quiet people, too. It seems to me that those who are quiet are often a wealth of insight when you finally get them to open up. Their years of listening pay off in terms of depth of spirit.

Several years ago I was shocked to read that a group of psychiatrists determined that shyness in children is a psychological condition sometimes worthy of counseling and maybe medication. It took my breath away. I was a shy child, our children were all shy, and some of our grandchildren are shy. I certainly never considered it a psychological condition. In fact, I've always believed that many of the children who sit back quietly and absorb the world around them gain great knowledge for their futures. I remember teachers of Garrison Keillor being amazed, based on his years in school, that he became the presenter and performer he did since he spent much of his time so quietly. Maybe that is why on Prairie Home Companion Keillor advertises Powdered Milk Biscuits as a product "for shy people so they can find the courage to get up and do what needs to be done."

I often wonder if we are born different kinds of people. Are there people born social who simply love interacting with others and know how to reach out in a crowd of strangers? Are there people who are innately shy, who would rather talk to one person in the corner of a room and who aren't able to move around the gathering talking to the crowds? Is it nature that makes us the way we are? I think about that as I watch others move among so many people with such ease.

Yet maybe nurture as well as nature has a role here. I grew up alone socially, although I'm not sure that is wholly to blame for my inability to mix easily. When I was young, we lived on a busy street in a bigger city with few children around to interact with. So, I read books. I was crazy about books back then and now, buried in them during the quiet spots in my life. I remember with passion so many of the books I loved when I was young. *Caddie Woodlawn* and her adventures in the wild woods of Wisconsin. The growing up of the sensitive girl Frances in *A Tree Grows in Brooklyn*. The deeper meanings of race and humanity in *The Adventures of Huckleberry Finn*. The despair and the hope laid bare in the words of Anne Frank. The meaning of integrity in *To Kill a Mockingbird*. In those young years, I read and read and read. One summer, I read 100 books. It was my door to adventures, and a link to the commonality of all people.

In all of my reading, I don't think I was really sad or understood that most children were out playing in the streets in neighborhoods abounding with kids. I loved my books, I loved riding my bike, I loved my quiet room. I was an early morning riser who would get up at dawn and ride my bike for hours, something we certainly wouldn't let our young children do alone today. But it was different, more trusting times and I remember those bike rides as being a gentle start to my days.

I came across a book the other day in my basement stash of books that I had when I was in middle school. It was called *A Friend is Someone Who Likes You*. The book must have been written for the shyer among us because its words comforted with its gentle reminders that a dog, a cat, a brook, a tree, and the wind can be a friend. I opened that long ago book and read its words, "The wind can be a friend too. It sings soft songs to you at night when you are sleepy and feeling lonely...."

I guess we are who we are, whether we are born that way or whether it comes from nurture. It's a funny thing about introverts, though. Susan Cain points out in *Quiet,* that they often learn those things that allow them, as Keillor says, "to do what needs to be done." They learn to do public speaking. They run for office. They get in front of gatherings to run meetings. And it is said that it is often very shy people who perform in plays, or sing in front of audiences, or give lectures. Barbra Streisand speaks of her terror before she sings in front of a crowd. She of the incredible voice. It's a wonder.

Cain has twenty questions in *Quiet* that let readers determine whether they are introverts or extroverts or somewhere in between. Of the twenty questions, I answered almost all as an introvert would. Which is okay. Because the one thing we know for sure is that the world is a richer place for having both introverts and extroverts. How wonderful that there are people who can get up and converse with a crowd and lead groups with their passion. How wonderful that there are people who can sit quietly alone in rooms for hours and read and think and develop new creations. How fortunate we are for the diversity of people and life and interest that abounds around us.

So, here's to the quiet and the not-so-quiet, the shy and the bold, the leaders and the followers - and to the richness that such diversity brings to this immensely complicated and incredibly precious journey that we travel together.

Rocks, Inner and Outer

There it was. At my feet. Suddenly and beautifully. A rock in the sand, a gift of white and green, cracked and sparkling up to me. A message almost, it seems on this pensive day. A gift from the waves.

I pick it up. This rock looks out of place here among the rougher, grayer rocks, as if it had been lifted and dropped capriciously from some place unknown. It is out of sync with its fellow rocks. I place it gently in my pocket, allowing it to bump against me as I walk, a gift for me for the days that lay ahead.

I have always been drawn to rocks. I remember picking up rocks almost wherever we went when I was little. I was most taken by those along beaches that were worn so smooth that they were shiny, glazed with the water of the lake or ocean. Sometimes, I would carry a small rock along with me and hold on to it for luck on lonesome days. Even now, I sometimes keep a smooth stone in my pocket. I actually have a jar of rocks on my desk. Do I keep them there to remind me of the rocky places? Do I have them on my desk to remind me of the stones among them that a group of peace advocates brought to my office one day? Am I nostalgic for the early days of childhood and how I was, in those faraway times, so close to the earth, the land, the water?

I came across the following among old writings of mine, "I hold the rock inside my hand, and it is cool and formed and beautiful. I, who have never felt quite finished, stare at the perfection of its lines, and hope for transformations yet to come."

Except for geologists, for years I never knew anyone but me who likes rocks so. Then, in recent years I've coincidentally come across several rock lovers, rock hounds they call themselves. It reminds me that we're never alone in the spaces we inhabit.

126

Geologists will tell you that our planet Earth is made mostly of rock that is millions of years old. The core of our earth is metal and around that is a thick layer of melted rock. The outer layer of earth is solid rock. No wonder rocks are so much a part of our psyches.

There are children's story books about rocks. My favorite lines from "If You Find a Rock" by Peggy Christian are these that conclude the book. "If you find a rock – a rock that's not a skipping rock, or a chalk rock, or a resting rock, or a wishing rock – that's not a splashing rock, or a sifting rock, or a worry rock, or a hiding rock – that's not even a climbing rock or a crossing rock, or a fossil rock, or a walking rock, but you like it anyway, because it reminds you of a place, or a feeling, or someone important, then you have found a memory rock, and sometimes those are the best rocks of all."

I have lots of memory rocks.

Years ago, I used to teach creative writing sessions to young children, and I'd usually end the experience by holding up a rock to the group. It is actually a particularly plain rock, gray, mottled, and pocked....nothing that anyone would pick up on a path to take with them. I would hold the rock up to the students and ask them for descriptive words, and I would hear back just what I expected....bumpy, dark, spotted, plain. Then I would turn the geode around to the side that is cracked open, a side that reveals a sparkling wonder, a cavern full of diamond-looking crystals.

I'm not certain where I got this rock. It is not like the museum store rocks that are sliced neatly in half and polished, but is instead a rough rock that is simply broken open in its natural state. And there it is, I always thought, a simple statement of reality, the inner gifts of light inside the plainness of life, the inspiration buried in routine, the beauty inside of the beast.

I think the students were a bit surprised by the rock's inside because the rock itself is so nondescript. I asked them why they thought I shared this rock with them, and, as young as they were, their insight was deep. "You can't always judge what's on the inside by what's on the outside." "Some ugly things are really very pretty." And, my favorite from a quiet little boy who didn't do well in school, "Maybe we have more inside of us than other people can see." Out of the mouths of babes....

I am at a low point in life now, and maybe that's why this rock makes me wonder.

I reach into my pocket and take out my memory rock from the beach. Had some wanderer like myself, thinking of her own sorrow, left it for a kindred traveler? Or did it drop from a bag unbeknownst to the carrier? Or was it simply from this place, but did not quite fit, this rock, cracked in some deep place, cooled by events it could not change.

And so this memory rock will stay with me and be a reminder of what we can yet discover when we too are lost and damaged.

The inner gifts among the cracks of who we are.

Horoscopes and Hope

I read my horoscope in the newspaper almost every day. It's not that I really believe in horoscopes, more that I often like their messages, suggestions and (sometimes) hopefulness. I mentally discard the ones that are not helpful, and I embrace the ones that feel right for me. Today was a day for embracing.

My horoscope read, "Go back to basics and keep things simple. Revisit your dreams and reconsider the possibilities. An honest assessment will help you bridge the gap between satisfaction and disappointment. Strive for betterment."

"The gap between satisfaction and disappointment." Now there's a phrase that resonates throughout literature and history. John Ciardi wrote of it, "The best of a man is what he thought of and could not be," and "We all live our lives in honor of the most possible lie." And there was Carl Sandburg writing of hope, "This reaching is alive yet for lights and keepsakes."

We all have it inside of ourselves, this striving for our most authentic selves, for meaning, and for those "lights and keepsakes beyond any hunger or death." We want to believe that there are still possibilities, that better days lie ahead, and that there are dreams that can yet come true.

I heard an interview recently with John Ramsey. He is the father who years ago lost a teenage daughter in an automobile accident, and a decade later lost another young daughter, Jon Benet, in a home invasion. More recently, his wife Patsy died of cancer. Yet he spoke somewhat somberly of the need to continue living and to believe that there can be good days ahead. He calls that belief, "the definition of hope."

Hope. The will to believe in tomorrow despite the obstacles, despite the sadness in our own histories, despite the pain. Jesse Jackson, Sr. calls it, "keeping hope alive." That is not always an easy task, this keeping hope alive, yet without hope nothing is possible. As Langston Hughes wrote is his beautiful poem *Dreams*, "Hold fast to dreams/For if dreams die/Life is a broken-winged bird/That cannot fly./Hold fast to dreams/For when dreams go/Life is a barren field/Frozen with snow."

Not too long ago, I was fortunate enough to interview a high school principal who is interesting for both his educational ideas and his view of life within a context of success. He encourages young people to look toward the ways that they can succeed in the years ahead of them. While that would be inspirational coming from anyone, it is especially so coming from this particular principal since he has been confined to a wheelchair since 1977.

He was just 16 years old when he had a waterskiing accident in which he lost his balance, was flung at 40 miles an hour, and hit rocks. He broke his neck and has been paralyzed from the neck down ever since. It was devastating for him and he now reflects that no one would have criticized him if he had decided to limit his horizons from then on, to discontinue his schooling, to spend the rest of his life in narrow confines.

And yet, while paralysis could have effectively ended the story for this talented man, he instead developed a mindset that allowed him to move forward. "Life is what it is," he told me. "I had a choice. Either I could make the most of my life or I could sit back and be a victim. I have tried to live with the idea that life is better lived and appreciated by celebrating each day rather than by wallowing in one's own despair." While he knows from experience that this isn't always easy, it makes him someone with a real life message.

He went on to become a teacher, an educational administrator, a parent, and the author of five books. When I asked him what advice he gives young people, he spoke of what he calls his 'life mantra.' "I believe in success," he says. "I believe that everybody can win at something. Young people need to find that something and celebrate it. We can be great, and that is what great looks like."

The great tennis legend Arthur Ashe once spoke profoundly of his own success when he said, "To achieve greatness, start where you are, use what you have, do what you can." And that is what Arthur Ashe did, it's what the high school principal has done, and it's what we all can aspire to do. As Kristin Jongen once wrote, "Perhaps strength doesn't reside in having never been broken, but in the courage to be strong in the broken places."

Last week, a reader wrote to me about making our way through dark times to a place of hope. He wrote about a story (which some claim is an urban legend) in which the great violin virtuoso, Yitzhak Perlman, was performing a violin concerto when a violin string suddenly broke. Supposedly, Perlman paused briefly and then continued to play the piece with only three strings. At the end of the concert, the audience gave him a standing ovation. Lowering his bow he turned toward the audience and said, "Our job is to make music with what remains."

True or not, this story suggests that keeping our mind positive matters. It is not always easy, this making music with what remains, but some show us that it can be done. As today's horoscope reminds us, "Go back to basics and keep things simple. Revisit your dreams."

The world is still ahead of us. Consider the possibilities.

Invincible Summer

I get SAD. Well, everyone gets sad sometimes. But I actually get SAD, otherwise known as Seasonal Affective Disorder. For years, I didn't know what was wrong with me. From adolescence on, I always believed that everything that went wrong in my life went wrong in January and February. I never knew why, but I was convinced that I was jinxed for those two months. I used to speculate as to the reasons. I wondered if it was my January birthday that spun me off course. Or maybe it was a post-holiday letdown. Or maybe it was the gloom of winter.

Yet, like so many people at low points in their journeys, I kept most of my wondering to myself and was convinced that it was just me, alone in this, strangely afflicted with a curse during the Januarys and Februarys of my life. In fact, I remember thinking as a young adult that I should just hide away in those two months, stay away from people, and hibernate like the bears.

And then, somewhere in my 30s, a liberating things occurred. I was listening to a news report which referred to a diagnosis identified as SAD, Seasonal Affective Disorder. It was first formally recognized and named by Dr. Norman E. Rosenthal in 1984 as a condition that affects individuals primarily in northern climates in the winter when the lack of ultraviolet light results in depression and mood disorders. And, since that time, SAD has become a well-understood condition ranging in incidence in the U.S. from a low of 1.4% among the Florida population to a high of 9.7% among the New Hampshire population. That is almost one in every ten people in New Hampshire and other northern states who suffer from SAD.

I remember how, upon hearing of the report, I sat down at the kitchen table and felt something between relief and eureka. I suddenly identified with the boundless legions of people who finally get a name for their condition and feel at last validated, at last understood. Now I knew it wasn't a trick of my mind, or a January-February curse, or hypochondria. It was something real.

And, like a puzzle that falls into place, the pieces all made sense. In the cold of winter, I stay inside. My favorite physical activities are biking and walking, things I rarely do in winter. And, for most of the years of my life, I was confined to Wisconsin for the duration of the winter. All of these things added up to a lack of sunlight, a lack of UV light. So, despite my belief that in our culture we over-diagnose, over-label, and over-medicate, there was nonetheless relief from this new understanding. Now I knew that there were things I could do about my January-February problem. For those who may share this issue, below are a few things I learned.

* When it is not frigid on these winter days, it is good to go out and take a daily walk. Walking not only helps SAD, but strengthens our bones and our muscles. And I find that I don't even get cold as easily after I come back from walks.

* If you have the luxury of going away even briefly in winter, try for a visit to sunnier climes. It can get you through the worst of it and sustain you until the advent of longer days.

* If you can't leave the darkness of winter, go online and order one of the phototherapy lights that are specially designed for those of us who fade like flowers without the sunshine we need. This disorder is, in truth, a poignant reminder of the interplay between light and darkness in our lives, and the importance of light, inner and outer, in our journeying.

* Talk to others about SAD. Talk to family members, friends, or counselors and you may realize that we are all in this together, making our way within a community of fellow travelers. Robert Fulghum has a wonderful essay about how we often wade in the waters of our own aloneness when there are resources that could help us. He called it, "standing knee deep in a river and dying of thirst." It is important for us to understand that, whatever we face, we are never alone in these things. Never.

Whether or not you have SAD, it is still true that we often find ourselves on uphill pathways in this journey when we are faced with our own hardships and sorrows. A minister friend reminds us that we are all broken, and that there is a unique beautiful to the mosaic of ourselves that results from that brokenness, if we are brave enough to endure.

Writer and philosopher Albert Camus once wrote, "In the depths of winter, I learned that there was within me an invincible summer." And so we seek to embrace the invincible summer within ourselves and to move forward, despite the hardships. That is a mighty lesson indeed, this lesson from the light, this lesson from the darkness. This lesson from SAD.

Zen Answers

Today, as I waited at a stoplight, I noticed a sign in a downtown window that read, "If you cannot find it inside yourself, where will you go for it?" As I was pondering that sign, an angry motorist blared his horn loudly at another driver who had waited too long to begin when the stoplight turned to green. The odd juxtaposition of the two encounters led me to wonder. If the answers are really inside of ourselves, why are we so often unable to live more at peace with ourselves and with others?

I have a friend who would tell me that the question posed by the sign is a perfect reflection of Zen Buddhist philosophy, that the answer is the things itself, i.e., the flower, the cloud, the rock, the sunrise — that the answers we need are indeed inside all things, including ourselves.

I think about the answers I need, and they don't seem to be inside myself. I consider a current life dilemma and realize that I have turned it over and over again in my mind, and I don't find the answers, despite my best intentions. If I am able to find it inside myself, why is it so hard to discover?

I drive down to the lake in this storm-filled weather to watch the waves, and they are crashing against the rocks on this tumultuous day with the wind blowing hard and the clouds changing shapes. Watching the view, I think what an incredible gift to have Lake Michigan right here in all of its splendor, not looking that much different than the ocean I would watch when we lived in California. Wave upon wave crash against these rocks in an unbelievable display, splashing water against the car windows. How complete it feels to sit here and just watch the waves, my mind free of all things, seeming almost part of their motions, cleansed of the concerns that drove me here to think. And now I know that maybe this is what Zen means.

Maybe it is enough to watch waves hitting rocks and to feel a part of those waves.

Maybe it is enough to watch the seagulls flying freely, in balance with their world.

Maybe it is enough to see the clouds changing shapes, letting the storm determine their picture.

Maybe it is enough to feel the wind touching all things with their cool fingers.

Maybe it is enough to wake up each morning with a grateful breath without moving on to concerns that have not yet arrived.

Maybe it is enough to live every moment of the moments we are given.

As I sit by the waves, I grow aware that it is time to drive away, back to the good life I have which nonetheless demands a full measure of who I am. This pause by the waves did little to take away the real life decisions that I must make. Still, I know that this pause did make a difference because it served as a reminder that there's always the lake, always the wind, always the waves, and always each moment to stop inside of and to simply embrace.

And so, in this sweet and complicated journey we are on, maybe sometimes that is the answer. The things themselves. It is so Zen.

New Beginnings

It is spring now, a time of new beginnings, awakening spirits, and a growing light in our lives. It is also that time of year when many people ponder retirement, consider the paths they are on, and reflect on new ones they could travel. It is that time of year.

According to statistics, 76 million people will turn 65 over the next two decades. That's almost 10,000 people per day. And statistics indicate that turbulence can often accompany retirees when they leave their work life.

A few years back, I retired from a position that was extremely busy, very time consuming, always interesting, and sometimes stressful. At the time, I thought that retirement was the right decision for me as I reflected on having more time to read books, to write, to play with grandkids, to see new sights, and to just pause when I wanted to. But even following that decision there were times when I didn't know if I had done the right thing. I guess that, as thinking people, we know that retirement is an enormous crossroads and we question ourselves.

Not long ago I read that recent retirees are returning to work in record numbers. Some of that may be the economy, but it also poses larger questions as well. How does a person decide about life changes? How do we know at any stage of our journey, and especially in the final decades, how to best expend our remaining time and our energy? How do we balance continuous activity against having the time to slow down and appreciate things more?

Given recent reflection, I now better understand the value of a job. A job keeps us on our toes, gives us a purpose, provides for a busy schedule, helps us connect with others, and generally provides our lives with a focus. I also know the value of not having a job. A fluid schedule allows us time to pursue new adventures, to create our own vocation, to venture out or stay in bed all day, to read, take walks, see friends, work for causes, and sometimes just slow down enough to notice the peace of a windy day, a quiet rain, or a new spring flower. I have a retired friend whose response to everyone's question, "So what are you doing now that you're retired?" is simply, "Whatever I want to do." Still, the question is a valid one. And perhaps the dilemma of life is that we seem often to have to choose one path or the other, akin to the ongoing philosophical debate surrounding the value of the active life versus the life of contemplation.

I have been at times in my life a career volunteer, and I still think of those efforts as some of the finer of my lifetime. I remember serving meals to the homeless, helping for years with multiple education-related efforts, serving on our local school board, and working for non-profit causes. And I remember other efforts like teaching adjunct or working freelance encouraging young people to read and write. Occasionally, former students would walk up to me in a mall or store and tell me that my efforts really made a difference in their lives. And, as teachers everywhere will tell you, it remains stunning when this happens. I remember the words of Helen Keller, "You never know the difference you make in the lives of others when you overcome your own obstacles, whatever those obstacles might be."

And so the question of being intentional in the choices we make about how we spend our energies as we get older is a fairly important one, especially since time seems to accelerate as we age. I often reflect on the fact that Laura Ingalls Wilder published her Little House on the Prairie books when she was 65. That Grandma Moses began painting in her 70s. That Charles Darwin was 50 when he published *On the Origin of Species*. That Colonel Saunders was in his 60s when he started the KFC chain. While we may not have the wherewithal of these individuals, we cannot know what is possible if we don't begin.

The briefness and the beauty of this journey is profound. And so we weigh our choices intentionally as we get older, hoping as we do that we are able to leave something lasting, some legacy in words, in deeds, in connections. For not to honor the precious gift of time would be a tragedy of major proportions.

As we navigate the waters of what to do next and how to balance competing demands in life and in retirement, we have to figure it out as we go. The challenge is to keep both activity and contemplation alive within the context of a rewarding life. And doubt will always be a part of the big picture, whatever we decide to do. In a quote from Franz Kafka's diaries he writes, "If we knew we were on the right road, having to leave it would mean endless despair. But we are on a road that only leads to a second one and then to a third one and so forth. And the real highway will not be sighted for a long, long time, perhaps never. And so we drift in doubt. But in compensation, the miracle remains forever possible."

And so, to those working, those retired, and those contemplating retirement, it might be best to focus on the ongoing joy in whatever roads we decide to travel. Perhaps the real miracle in this journey is, after all, the journey itself.

There are new beginnings to be found everywhere. We just need to discover them.

Spirituality

For years, I didn't go to church. I only attend now because I found a church with liberal enough views to accommodate my agnostic soul. When our children were young, we loosely attended a church we couldn't believe in, probably trying to ensure that they would grow up knowing the Christian reality of our culture and the profound goodness of Jesus. But, after our children were older, I didn't go to church, a reality at odds with my growing up years when every Sunday included worship. For years, my non-church attendance was a reality that felt right to my old, wisened soul. My philosophy had become so simple, a sort-of religion itself, I suppose –

  * Live a good life, a life that honors yourself and others.

  * Be grateful for each day of this sweet and simple existence.

  * Take care of this earth in its amazing beauty. Take years to enjoy it.

  * Be a peacemaker in these days of violence. Advocate hard for the world to know peace. Make peace in your own life.

  * Don't blame others. It's usually nobody's fault.

  * Forgive yourself. You know how hard you are trying.

  * Make your own reality, your own decisions, your own choices. The only thing we can change is ourselves.

  * Know joy, and work to find it.

  * In this world of cynicism, avoid cynics. The world is a glorious place, and most people are trying as hard as they know how to.

  * Find work that is meaningful to you and that gives meaning to the world.

  * Enjoy simple things. Picnic sandwiches. The hand of a child. Swings. Bicycles. A vase of dandelions. A glass of ice water. A juicy peach. The smile of an old person. The sound of waves.

* Embrace the diversity of life in all of its forms. We are our brother's keepers. We are our sister's keepers.

* Understand that nobody knows the answers. Plain and simple. No person knows. No church knows. No religion knows. Just understand that the answer to the riddle of our lives, the lives of those who have gone before us, and the lives of those to come after us is an inscrutable mystery that we are honored to be a part of.

* Believe that we, each of us, have only this moment we are in, that and nothing more. It is all that is promised us, this time. Knowing that makes the sweetness of our time so real. Enjoy. Live. Laugh. Love. It is what it is all about.

I guess the above is like being in a church for doubters who still believe in spirituality because digging into our deeper souls is all we can know and all we need to know. There's a Zen philosophy that speaks of the truth we find within. It is what I believe too – that what answers there are, we can find in inner places, in the deep recesses of our spirit. It is the unanswered questions that will always keep us seeking.

The Loss Of a Child

Jocelyn

"In loss, there are not words enough to explain."
— Author's Journal Entry

The End...
And Beginning Again

Sometimes we have to begin again during this complicated journey. In a way, this book for me is about an ending, and about trying to begin again. For some of us are forced to face the reality of thinking of our lives in terms of "before" and "after." "Was that before or after, Jocelyn died?," I sometimes stop and think to myself. There are those among us for whom the unthinkable happens. We get a phone call, or a stranger comes to the door, or a diagnosis is made, and it changes our lives. For some of us there was an ending, and then a search for a new way to begin. Again.

We have a friend who says that all of us are broken in many ways, damaged by that which life brings to us. But, he says, we make our legacy by what we do with that breakage, by the kaleidoscope created from the shards of our souls. And so, this book.

I wrote most of the previous essays in this volume before the tragic death of our younger daughter, and thus most of the prior essays are the product of the years when I felt so proud of our legacy of raising four brilliant, creative, kind young people. Since that night when our world broke into a million pieces, writing has been harder and it most often touches on the loss and heartbreak of her being gone. Still, she is with us. As Sir James Frazer once wrote, "The second principle of magic is that things which have once been in contact with each other continue to act on each other at a distance after the physical contact has been severed." We know the reality of that.

I am buoyed by that which helps us survive...our oldest daughter, her husband, and their three children...our older son and his daughter...our younger son and his wife…and my husband with whom I share the terror of that tragic night and the sorrow of missing a daughter who will never be with us again but who is in our hearts. I have these people who I love beyond imagining, as well as other family members, close friends, and the work that I do. And, of course, my writing.

And so I try to move forward, as Ciardi wrote, "in what light there is."

Water and Meditation

It is late fall, and I am alone at the beach. There are no joyful yelps of children jumping into waves. No siblings burying each other neck deep in sand. No sandcastle moats being filled with water. No mothers screaming into the expanse of the lake, "You are out too far! Move in closer."

There is a solitary figure walking at the far end of the beach, staring into autumn waves. Being myself a haunter of these sands of autumn, I understand that those who frequent these places this time of year usually come to be alone, to listen to the music of the waves, to make friends with the remaining seagulls, and, perhaps, to be in touch with their own buried wounds, their own inner brokenness. "Water and meditation," Herman Melville wrote, "are forever wedded." And so we sit and stare, drawn to the peace and the depth of water.

I am broken and wounded, alone at this site that carries the early chill of the winter soon to be upon us. I know winter well now for it lives within me since the summer death of our beautiful, smart, kind, sensitive, 32-year-old youngest daughter. The solitude of the beach feels right to me now, right for a notebook, a blanket, a thermos of cider, and for my unhealing wounds. It is a place made for pausing, for taking time to reflect, for reminding myself of the preciousness and ephemeral nature of what we have. I learned the hardest way possible that what we have can be gone in a sudden breath, and we can be left behind, bereft and barren and lost.

In the early 1900s, my grandmother, my mother's mother, lost her oldest son to spinal meningitis. Today's medicine could most likely have saved Raphael but the tools back in those days weren't available. He was only 16, an incredibly good looking young person, with sensitivity and intelligence and compassion written all over his face. Many years after Raphael died, an older sister of his said to me privately that grandma was never the same again after Raphael's death. I mentioned that to my mom years later, and she contested it. She said that her mother had gone forward to live with strength and joy and humor. That may be true but, having been where I've been, I resonate with my aunt's account. You never really heal from these things, I am learning. You just make a choice to keep taking one step after another, and you make a choice to try to stay grateful for those gifts that still abide. It is not enough, but it is something. I join my grandmother's league in this lonesome reality.

This time of year, I think of the legion of us, trying so hard to get through the holidays, the smiling faces of children, the brightness of Christmas trees, the colorful wrapped gifts, the continuous holiday carols, and the trappings of this joyous season of love. From my childhood through the childhoods of our children, I have always loved the holiday season. Still, this year I understand more than I ever have before how painful idyllic images can be for broken souls like mine.

To those who ask me how I'm doing, I reply the same thing, "I'm trying. I really am trying." And so I will, like those who carry similar wounds, try to get through the holidays with a measure of the joy and grace our daughter would have wanted us to have and that our loved ones deserve.

I was at a meeting last week where we were asked to say something we are grateful for. One woman said, "I am grateful for the ability to still be grateful." I don't know what her wounds are, but I know she couldn't have shared such a profound reflection without having some unhealed place within herself.

And so, for you and for me, I wish the same thing. May we retain the strength and the wisdom to be grateful even amidst the pain we endure. May we "welcome humbly the light and proudly the darkness," as e.e. cummings wrote.

Alone on the beach today, I remember that lesson borne out of water and meditation.

"Humbly the light and proudly the darkness."

We stumble along within a changing kaleidoscope of both realities.

My Morning Puppy, My Mourning Puppy

I don't know why I got a dog, much less a puppy. I am far older than the last time I had a puppy right after college, and I vaguely remember the problems with puppies. They chew things you don't want them to chew. They pee, and even worse, in the house until they finally figure out, months later, what you are asking them to do. They want to play all the time, especially when you want to sleep, a request that is easier when you have young children than when you are a busy middle-aged person.

Still, there he was staring up at me, all 4 pounds of him, fuzzy fur, big brown eyes, and a head that tipped when I talked to him. And so I acknowledged to myself what I knew the moment I first saw him, "He looks like he belongs with me." And thus he bounded, puppyhood and all, into my house and my life. Little Tucker.

Last night was our first night with him and I slept lightly, a flashback to the days when we had new babies. You listen for every sound. You don't want to miss them if they wake up. And, in the early morning hours, you hope that they will sleep just a little longer so that you can have some morning time alone. It seldom happens.

Of course, I know why I really have Tucker. He is my morning dog of my mourning days. Our beautiful, bright, kind, sensitive, smiling 32-year old daughter died and I am doing all that I can to survive, to carry on, to find a new normal. The truth is, I draw upon every strength I can muster, feeling most often like a walking, talking wound. Pain is so close to the surface that I can cry at anything, a mention of green bean casseroles, a song from Beauty and the Beast, the glimpse of a yellow rose. Her favorite things.

Still, I am pretty good at trying, good even at "pretend normal." Most of the time. People sometimes comment that I seem to be doing well, and I know why they say that. I can do meetings, or small groups of friends, or small family gatherings. And when I can't, I just leave for home or for her grave where I can let the tears flow in solitude, the memories wash over me, and her absence burn like a fire inside.

Tucker is one way I am trying to survive. "A puppy and a warm blanket," as my friend commented. I can hold him and cry into his abundance of soft fur and allow him to distract me, especially in the early morning hours, the alonest time in the world. Anna Quindlen wrote some haunting words in a novel about loved ones dying, "The worst thing about losing someone you love, is that you lose them all over again every morning."

Jocelyn loved dogs, just as she loved all things innocent and vulnerable and damaged. It was why she was so good at what she did, working with autistic children. We have a friend who reminds us that we are all broken in various ways and that it is what we do with that brokenness that forms the kaleidoscope of our lives. And so the vulnerability and sensitivity within my daughter resonated with the same qualities in the autistic children she served. I made a scrapbook of the letters sent to us from fellow therapists and families of autistic children. They wrote incredible things. "Jocelyn saved my daughter's life." "The moment Jocelyn walked into our home and took our son's hands in her own, she became a part of our family." "Jocelyn is the person I role model when I do therapy with my students." And this, from a child, "I know I am only 13 but I love Jocelyn soooo much. I know her family misses her but of anyone who isn't her family, I will miss her the most." We have hundreds of letters and writings in the Jocelyn scrapbook, precious words of tribute from the autism community.

Last spring when our 17-year old dog Toby became ill and couldn't eat anymore, we were told by our vet that the most merciful thing to do was to put him to sleep. Jocelyn phoned us and asked that we not do anything until she could stop over to see him. When she arrived, she did a thing true to her nature. She cried and asked if I could leave her alone for awhile so that she could talk with Toby. I left and she spent an hour by herself with him. She cared so much. Those are words I considered putting on her gravestone, simple and clear. "She cared so much." It may have been, ultimately, her downfall.

I glance down at Tucker as he begins to chew my shoe, another bad habit we will try to break him of. Still, he will be good for me, this morning dog of my mourning days. Not to help me forget, because forgetting such a person would be a tragedy of monumental proportions. But to help me remember the joy of a life that, while too short, was well-lived, full of laughter, alive with dreams, and filled with the legacy of the many children she helped.

Jocelyn would have loved Tucker, and he would have loved her. She would be glad I have him now. I just wish she could be here to meet him.

She would walk into our house with her contagious smile, she would laugh her bubbling laugh, and I would be so glad to hear it.

Her laughter that will echo forever down the long hallways of my memory.

Thank You, Marcy

It was November and I was out shopping casually in the store, grabbing a few holiday items during the pre-season time before the real craziness of it all would become too overwhelming.

I used to love the holidays. Since the death of our youngest daughter, the season is much more complicated now. My spirit sometimes bristles with it all, the music, the merriment, the colored lights. Still, since so much of my life is "pretend normal," I carry on as best I can. Our daughter was a joyous, smart and sweet soul, and I almost hear her sometimes nudging me on. "Go ahead, mom, you can do it." She would have smiled her radiant smile at me. It's that and her tender words that I miss the most, I think. And her humor.

I don't discount my many blessings. We have loving children, an older daughter and her husband, an older son, a younger son and his wife, and amazing grandchildren. I have a supportive husband who I lean on, and close friends. Still, the season is a challenge to the blow we've been dealt, the loss we live with always.

Anyway, there I was, just shopping, and a stranger approached me. "Is your name Linda?," she asked from a kind face.

"Yes." I smiled back at her.

"I'm Marcy. Didn't you once write a column for the newspaper?," she asked.

I nodded.

"I miss it," she said with a gentleness. "Each Sunday, I open the paper up, hoping it will be there. Could you start writing it again?"

As old as I get, I never cease to be amazed by how good people are, and how much of kindness we see in the eyes of others.

154

I thanked Marcy and answered as honestly as I could. "It is so hard since our younger daughter died. She used to read my columns before I submitted them and she would encourage me, edit words, and rank which ones I should submit." I sighed.

What I didn't tell Marcy was the rest of it. I didn't tell her that when something so terrible happens there is so much you can't write about. You can't write with gratitude about the knowledge that comes with growing older. You can't write about the everyday adventures of an active family without remembering what is gone. And you don't want to write of your continuing sorrow. So you get frozen in time. I often wonder if others who have lost children get frozen in time, too. We are seldom alone in our own tragedies, our own realities.

"I understand," she nodded. "Still…" Her words trailed off and then rebounded once again with energy. "I kept your columns, and I have one in my nightstand next to my bed. I read it often."

And so she prompted gently again. "Try. If you can. Try."

I looked at her and I recalled why I liked doing the column in the first place. It made me feel connected, one with all who cry and laugh, who suffer and celebrate, who just plain live through this journey.

In life we sometimes encounter and, if we are lucky, we sometimes are ourselves those people who encourage, support, and prod others to be their best and most authentic selves.

A father tells his son, "You are so talented. You can do this."

"This is remarkable work," a teacher tells her student. "Wow."

And Abraham Lincoln's words from so many years ago remind us also that we have within ourselves "the better angels of our nature."

So, here's to Marcy who told a stranger who was out holiday shopping to carry on despite it all. And here's to all of the Marcys who help us to grow, to believe in ourselves, and to find the better angels of our natures. Those who remind us to keep walking, even when it's only putting one foot in front of the other, even when it's only one step at a time. Even when it's only a beginning.

This New Years, perhaps we can find, or perhaps we can be, the Marcys in the lives of others and in our own lives.

It's a gift of today to last far into the future.

For that and more, thank you to my Marcy and to all of the Marcys out there, wherever you are. You lift us up, you propel us forward into a new year and a new future.

And you help us to believe. Once again.

A Daughter's Legacy

When our youngest son was in his early years of middle school, he spent one summer watching the movie *Dead Poets Society* about once every week. I remember asking him why he was so intrigued with it. He didn't elaborate, but his one-sentence response spoke volumes. "It just means so much," he said with a very intense earnestness. "It just means so much."

The 2014 passing of Robin Williams seemed almost more than the nation could bear. From his movies to his comedic standup routines to his TV and radio interviews, the range and genius of this man was profound. And yet he was so human, so kind, so vulnerable like ourselves. We feel we knew him.

Like my son, I also loved *Dead Poets Society*, and I remember my amazement also at *Good Morning Vietnam*. How could he do that, I wondered as we left that theatre so many years ago. What kind of mind can have that quick wit, talent, compassion? His subsequent movies revealed even more of his humor and depth. I remember the scene in *Good Will Hunting* when he repeats over and over again to his client, "It isn't your fault, it isn't your fault" until the patient releases his pain in tears. How often those with depression could benefit from such words. And perhaps on some level, Robin Williams was also saying that phrase to himself as well. Perhaps he understood, even early on, his own demons.

In our family, we have the genetics for depression. A commentator said this week of Robin Williams, "He struggled in an ongoing battle with profound depression." I know the reality of that battle myself for I've seen it and felt it firsthand. I know the reluctance of people to discuss mental health issues. So many people over the years spoke of Robin's addiction issues but only seldom of his depression. I know the helplessness of those who love people in this battle and the futility they feel in trying to ease the pain. There seems so little we can do.

In 2012, our daughter died much as Williams did. Like the nation with Williams' death, we also were stunned into disbelief and silence, left with unhealing wounds. Like Robin, our daughter was a person with a quick smile and endearing sense of humor. She was sensitive and kind and, like Robin, she had an intense seriousness about things that mattered, in her case the work she embraced with her autistic students. Just as Robin's family, we knew of her sadness but her beautiful smile and work made her decision something unbelievable to us and to those who knew her. As one of her friends said after her death, "She hid her pain well." And so I resonated with what the Williams family experienced. Sometimes there are no words. We simply have to carry on.

Robin Williams' wife gave a poignant statement following his death. She asked that the world remember Robin not for his death, but for the humor and the meaning of his work. It is a request I make of myself every single day - that I continue to focus on the joy, the depth, and the legacy of our dear girl's life.

They leave scars on our hearts that time does not erase or heal, these intense, brilliant, hurting ones. And so we thank you, Robin Williams, for all the gifts you have given us. And we thank you, our dear daughter. You are not, and will never be, forgotten.

Your lives mattered.

Reincarnation

When I emailed my friend Sue and told her that I was "in a slump" and couldn't get together for a visit, her response was rapid and humorous. "And what are you learning there in your slump?" Sue emailed back, tongue-in-cheek. While I smiled at her response, my mind immediately flashed back to another friend I had many years ago. Elizabeth believed in reincarnation, believed that we are reborn continuously into new lives and that the message of being alive through hard times is that we have things to learn from every experience we encounter.

While I don't myself believe in reincarnation, I was struck nonetheless by this notion of life as a continuous rebirth of ideas and regeneration. I recalled how Elizabeth had lived her life so intentionally even though she was at a particularly painful part of her personal journey. "What am I supposed to be learning?," she would ask herself. "What am I supposed to be getting out of this?"

How often do we ourselves ask this, especially at the difficult times of our lives? Like Job, we sometimes wonder, "Why? Why me?" And the answers are as silent as the darkness.

Being in a dark place myself and seeking answers, I thought back to my long-ago friend Elizabeth and her response to her pain. What did *she* learn in her slump? Well, she decided to take a journey, all alone, to the southwest and its deserts. At that time, she couldn't explain why she wanted to go there, although she knew why she wanted to go alone. It was a journey of self-exploration after many years of the cacophony of family and kids and schedules.

After Elizabeth arrived back home, she told me that she believed that her journey to the desert was prompted by her own sense of dryness and her feeling of being in an arid desert of her own making. Life has its ironies, though. Not knowing much about the desert, she left for the southwest in April of that year. What she found was tremendously healing. She discovered that, far from being dry and dull, the desert was ablaze in flowers of many colors, many shapes, many hues reaching for the sun.

And there, in that slump she was in, she learned a truth. Even in the most arid places in our lives, rebirth and regeneration still can be. If these driest of plants can herald joy, who are we not to believe in possibilities? There is a wonderful poem by Byrd Baylor called "The Desert is Theirs." Its words are haunting and the ending profound, "That's why every desert thing knows when the time comes to celebrate. Suddenly...all together, it happens. Cactus blooms yellow and pink and purple. The Papagos begin their ceremonies to pull down rain. Every plant joins in. Even the dry earth makes a sound of joy when the rain touches. Hawks call across the canyons. Children laugh for nothing. Coyotes dance in the moonlight. Where else would Desert People want to be?"

Perhaps because of my current "slump," I was interested in a Time Magazine article on new research that claims that animals grieve. They wrote of elephants who come together sometimes for days as in a funeral for the one who has died, of a dog who returned daily for ten years to the train station where he had always met his now deceased owner, even of whales who seem to hum a song of mourning for the one who is gone.

Reading the article, I thought back to 2006, the year that my younger brother Don passed away of cancer. After he died his dog Maggie (not a growler), would sit on Don's side of the bed at night and growl at anyone, even the kids, who would try to sit in his place. Maggie was waiting for her friend to come back, a longing shared by those of us who loved him. Grief is, after all, probably the worst slump of all. How can we survive it? And what do we learn?

So to my dear friend Sue who emailed me, here are the things I am learning in my slump.

I am learning that keeping busy is all about survival. When we most want to crawl under the covers and die, that is just the time that we must get up, move around, make connections.

I am learning that there are wounds that will never heal, wounds that on some level you don't want to heal for fear of losing the memories in the process. And so you learn to embrace a sadness that will never be completely gone.

I am learning that no matter how much you have suffered through, there are so many others out there with their own sorrows who need what only fellow sufferers can provide. Whether their sorrows are greater, less, or equal to your own makes no difference at all. A person's suffering is their suffering, and sharing lightens the burden a bit.

And I am learning that there is a new depth of understanding that rises out of suffering, and that one of the greatest legacies of pain is empathy.

So thanks to my present-day friend who asked me what I am learning and thanks to my long-ago friend who taught me to keep searching for the message. In our own desert places, plants of beauty and spirit may yet bloom again.

And that, I guess, is a kind of reincarnation all of its own. To bloom again. The desert lets us know that it is possible.

You Know Who You Are

At the end of a book, authors often thank all of those who have helped them with their writing and their book. I am always in wonderment that they can do this since it would be impossible for me to name all of those writers, friends, and family who have helped me to write, advised me, and encouraged me to continue. And so I just say this — you know who you are. Thanks for nudging me forward in the writing journey. I could not have done it without you.

Made in the USA
Charleston, SC
03 April 2015